THE ROLE OF METAPHOR
IN ART THERAPY

ABOUT THE AUTHOR

Figure 1. Self-Portrait, Acrylic on Canvas, 36″ x 42″.

Bruce L. Moon, Ph.D., ATR-BC, is a member of the faculty and chair of the art therapy department at Mount Mary College in Milwaukee, Wisconsin. Formerly the director of the graduate program at Marywood University in Scranton, Pennsylvania, and the Harding Graduate Clinical Art Therapy Program in Worthington, Ohio, he has extensive clinical, administrative, and teaching experience. He holds a doctorate in creative arts with specialization in art therapy from Union Institute in Cincinnati, Ohio. Dr. Moon's current clinical practice is focused on the treatment of emotionally disturbed adolescents. He has lectured and led workshops at many colleges, universities, conferences, and symposia in the United States and Canada.

Dr. Moon is the author of *Existential Art Therapy: The Canvas Mirror; Essentials of Art Therapy Education and Practice; Introduction to Art Therapy: Faith in the Product; Art and Soul: Reflections on an Artistic Psychology; The Dynamics of Art as Therapy with Adolescents;* and *Ethical Issues in Art Therapy.* He is editor of Working with Images: The Art of Art Therapists, and co-edited Word Pictures: The Poetry and Art of Art Therapists. Moon's many years of experience in clinical and educational settings, coupled with his interdisciplinary training in theology, art therapy, education, and creative arts, inspire his provocative theoretical and practical approach to the multiple roles and forms of metaphor in art therapy.

Author's Note

The clinical vignettes in this book are, in spirit, true. In all instances, details are fictional to ensure the confidentiality of persons with whom I have worked. The case illustrations and artworks presented are amalgamations of many specific situations. My intention is to provide realistic accounts of an art therapist's work with metaphors while also protecting the privacy of individuals.

THE ROLE OF METAPHOR
IN ART THERAPY

Theory, Method, and Experience

By

BRUCE L. MOON, PH.D., ATR-BC

CHARLES C THOMAS • PUBLISHER, LTD.
Springfield • Illinois • U.S.A.

Published and Distributed Throughout the World by

CHARLES C THOMAS • PUBLISHER, LTD.
2600 South First Street
Springfield, Illinois 62794-9265

©2007 by CHARLES C THOMAS • PUBLISHER, LTD.

ISBN-13: 978-0-398-07752-5 (hard)
ISBN-10: 0-398-07752-5 (hard)
ISBN-13: 978-0-398-07753-2 (pbk.)
ISBN-10: 0-398-07753-3 (pbk.)

Library of Congress Catalog Card Number: 2007008499

With THOMAS BOOKS *careful attention is given to all details of manufacturing
and design. It is the Publisher's desire to present books that are satisfactory as to their
physical qualities and artistic possibilities and appropriate for their particular use.*
THOMAS BOOKS *will be true to those laws of quality that assure a good name
and good will.*

Printed in the United States of America
MM-R-3

Library of Congress Cataloging in Publication Data

Moon, Bruce L.
  The role of metaphor in art therapy : theory, method, and experience / by
Bruce L. Moon.
      p. cm.
  Includes bibliographical references and index.
  ISBN-13: 978-0-398-07752-5 (hard)
  ISBN-10: 0-398-07752-5 (hard)
  ISBN-13: 978-0-398-07753-2 (pbk.)
  ISBN-10: 0-398-07753-3 (pbk.)
  1. Art therapy. 2. Metaphor. I. Title.
  [DNLM: 1. Art Therapy–methods. 2. Mental Disorders–therapy. 3.
Metaphor. WM 450.5.A8 M818r 2007]

RC489.A7M666 2007
616.89'1656--dc22   2007008499

FOREWORD

The profession of art therapy has faced identity battles since its formal beginnings some 50 years ago. In that time, art therapists
have defined and redefined theory and practice, struggled for recognition in the field of mental health, and asserted the efficacy of art as
therapy, art in therapy, and art psychotherapy. The function of art in
assessment, diagnosis, and treatment is debated within the profession
and challenged outside the profession. Other mental health practi-
tioners use art materials in therapy and assessment while licensure
bids, managed care, and insurance companies hold sway over who
gets treated and who provides the treatment.

Dr. Bruce Moon challenges the system in this text on metaphor in
art therapy. Moon engages children, adolescents, and adults in art
making, situating the therapeutic relationship directly in the artistic
dialogue. By Moon's definition, one cannot be an art therapist or be
doing art therapy unless engaged in one's own art making both in and
out of session. He is passionate in his philosophy that "the therapeutic
alliance is fostered when the focus is placed on the art process, [that]
the therapeutic relationship emerges from the shared experience of
client and therapist making art in the company of one another." In
addition to asserting that the relationship forms and transforms in this
shared experience, Moon believes that all artworks are metaphors of
the person who created them. He argues (and I agree) that art as a tool
in verbal therapy or as a means of diagnosis is not art therapy. For
Moon, art therapy involves the practice of creating personal metaphor
and advocating multiple meanings. He opposes the "systematic labeling and reductive interpretation of artwork" and speaks strongly to the
practice of talking to images, establishing a respectful conversation
with the artwork, and responding to imagery with story and poetry.
Dr. Moon has a way with story and metaphor, using them to help the

reader understand the process he describes throughout the text. He dubs himself "metaphoretician" and offers guidelines in his use of metaphor and the role of artist-therapist in art therapy.

Moon's assertions are rooted in the psychology of art, art therapy theory, and to a certain degree, the imaginal work of post-Jungian archetypal psychologists. Florence Cane (1951, 1983) and Edith Kramer (1971, 1986) give us roots in studio-based approaches to art therapy, and both note the artwork being representative of its creator. Mildred Lachman-Chapin (1979) writes of her own art making with clients as central to therapeutic process. Janie Rhyne (1973, 1994) describes work with clients and groups in which she actively participates with her group members in the art process and describes the art creations as speaking about the creator. In speaking of the art group, Rhyne states: "The added dimension of genuine contact and communication is the most essential part. . . . All of our training in techniques, structures, and methodology is meaningless sham unless we evoke and develop the reality of knowing and being known" (p. 167). Michael Franklin (1990) discusses the relevance of esthetics and empathy in looking at client artwork without judgment and in responding to the client through art making. Janis Timm-Bottos (2001) offers a furthering of the studio-based approach, alive and well in community-based centers today, where artists and art therapists work side-by-side, making art, exploring issues of transition, and listening metaphorically. Catherine Moon (2002) argues for the arts-based model of art therapy practice and the poetic response to the metaphoric language of the client.

Mala Betensky (1973, 1995) defines the phenomenological method of art therapy, noting the art product as "a phenomenon with its own structure" (1995, p. xi). She describes assisting the client in learning to see what is in the artwork and using precise verbal description, such that the connection between the artwork and the client's inner experience is recognized. Vija Lusebrink (1990) reminds us of the "multi-leveledness" (Kreitler & Kreitler, 1972) of meaning in a work of art and of the concept of isomorphism (Arnheim, 1974) that allows us to consider the relationship between the internal state of the artist and the external manifestation or interaction in the art media. Sandra Kagin and Lusebrink (Kagin, 1969; Kagin & Lusebrink, 1978; Lusebrink, 1990) also developed a continuum of expression and variables of artistic media, giving art therapists a structure by which they can understand and make decisions with regard to facilitating the client's process. The continuum and variables can be understood metaphorically and provide a theoretical basis for what Bruce Moon defines as our responsibility "to translate clients' metaphoric messages into theoretical understandings and treatment interventions that are appropriate within the therapeutic milieu."

Shaun McNiff (1992) discusses the process of talking to the artwork, establishing conversations between the creator and the art, and Rhyne suggests such interaction from within a Gestalt psychology framework. David Maclagan (2001) and Linney Wix (2000, 2003), among others, discuss the early traditions (in what is now called art therapy) of bringing art to people in different situations. Looking at the works of artists in psychiatric hospitals, convalescent wards, and educational settings (Hill, Adamson, Lydiatt, Simon, Edwards, Henzell, and Huntoon), and in concentration camps (Dicker-Brandeis), these authors define art therapy as firmly situated in a studio approach and note the importance, in fact necessity, of the therapist's experience as an artist who understands art making from the inside.

Metaphor is a difficult concept and often misunderstood. Mary Watkins (1976) states that it "takes a different eye to see. When we understand the secret that things are not only as they appear to common sensible perception, we find the need to nurture an uncommon kind of perception" (p. 12). Watkins (1981) also speaks to the necessity of the art therapist being in touch with his or her own art making, insisting that we must attend to our own images if we are to be available to the images of others. "We must write out our dreams, illustrate them, speak to their characters, paint spontaneously, seek for the images that determine our responses to others, to ourselves, our patients and our life" (p. 125). James Hillman (1977) speaks to the de-literalizing, sometimes humorous, sense of metaphor and the importance of admitting one's lostness in front of the image. In the works of Hillman (1981) and Berry (1982), metaphor is found in the precise description of the image, hearing that description metaphorically, discovering the necessity within the image, and making the image matter. If indeed as art therapists we are not about fixing, interpreting, or diagnosing the patient, but about art making and "being trusting enough to convey to another an openness to images" (Watkins, 1981, p. 121) in therapy, then we must "discover what the image wants and from that determine our therapy" (Berry, 1982, p. 78).

Bruce Moon adds to this ongoing dialogue in literature with concrete examples and dedication to the idea that therapy is in the art making of both therapist and client. He confirms the viability of the concepts of metaphor and art in therapy, offering case vignettes that clearly, and often poetically, describe a reliance on an intuitive grasp of situations and an improvisational way of working alongside clients. He discusses the reciprocal self-disclosure, the sharing of vulnerabilities, the shared journey, and the therapist and client coming to know each other in the mutual art-making process. His passion for his work is evident throughout the text, in his storytelling and his poetry, as well as in the more didactic and practical components of explaining the practice of art therapy.

JOSIE ABBENANTE
Laguna, New Mexico

REFERENCES

Arnheim, R. (1974). *Art and visual perception.* (Rev. ed.). Berkeley: University of California Press.

Berry, P. (1982). *Echo's subtle body: Contributions to an archetypal psychology.* Dallas, TX: Spring Publications.

Betensky, M. (1973). Patterns of visual expression in art psychotherapy. *Art Psychotherapy, 1,* 121–129.

Betensky, M. (1995). *What do you see: Phenomenology of therapeutic art expression.* London: Jessica Kingsley.

Cane, F. (1983). *The artist in each of us.* (Rev. ed.). Craftsbury Common, VT: Art Therapy Publications.

Franklin, M. (1990). The esthetic attitude and empathy: A point of convergence. *The American Journal of Art Therapy, 29*(2), 42–47.

Hillman, J. (1977). An inquiry into image. *Spring 1977,* 62–88.

Hillman, J. (1981). *Archetypal psychology: A brief account.* Dallas, TX: Spring Publications.

Kagin, S., & Lusebrink, V. (1978). The expressive therapies continuum. *Art Psychotherapy, 5*(3), 171–179.

Kramer, E. (1971). *Art as therapy with children.* New York: Schocken Books.

Kramer, E. (1986). The art therapist's third hand: Reflections on art, art therapy, and the society at large. *American Journal of Art Therapy, 24*(3), 71–86.

Kreitler, H., & Kreitler, S. (1972). *Psychology of the arts.* Durham, NC: Duke University Press.

Lachman-Chapin, M. (1979). Kohut's theories on narcissism: Implications for art therapy. *American Journal of Art Therapy, 19*(1), 3–9.

Lusebrink, V. (1990). *Imagery and visual expression in therapy.* New York: Plenum Press.

Maclagan, D. (2001). *Psychological aesthetics: Painting, feeling and making sense.* London: Jessica Kingsley.

McNiff, S. (1992). *Art as medicine: Creating a therapy of the imagination.* Boston: Shambala Press.

Moon, C. (2002). *Studio art therapy: Cultivating the artist identity in the art therapist.* London: Jessica Kingsley.

Rhyne, J. (1973). *The gestalt art experience.* Monterey, CA: Brooks/Cole.

Timm-Bottos, J. (2001). The heart of the lion: Joining community through art making. In M. Farrelly-Hansen (Ed.), *Spirituality and art therapy: Living the connection* (pp. 204–226). London: Jessica Kingsley.

Watkins, M. (1976). *Waking dreams.* Dallas, TX: Spring Publications.

Watkins, M. (1981). Six approaches to the image in art therapy. *Spring 1981,* 107–125.

Wix, L. (2000). Looking for what's lost: The artistic roots of art therapy: Mary Huntoon. *Art Therapy: Journal of the American Art Therapy Association, 17*(3), 168–176.

Wix, L. (2003). *Art in the construction of self: Three women and their ways in art, therapy, and education.* Unpublished dissertation, University of New Mexico, Albuquerque.

ACKNOWLEDGMENTS

I am indebted to many colleagues, teachers, and mentors who shaped my ideas on metaphors. Prominent among them are Dr. Edward Meyer, formerly a professor of homiletics at the Methodist Theological School in Ohio, and Don Jones, ATR, HLM. Dr. Meyer and Don helped lay the groundwork for my understanding of metaphors in stories and artworks.

My method and approach have been deeply influenced, both overtly and subtly, by many art therapists and related theorists. Among them are Pat Allen, Florence Cane, Shaun McNiff, Catherine Moon, Janie Rhyne, Bob Schoenholtz, and Mary Watkins. The writings of James Hillman have also inspired me. Without all the above contributions, this book would not have been possible.

I am grateful to the students at Mount Mary College who tolerated my rambling discussions of metaphors as this book took shape; their critical responses and constructive suggestions were insightful. I also want to express gratitude to my colleague, Dr. Lynn Kapitan, who read and commented on early drafts of the manuscript, and Ling Olaes, an aspiring art therapist who edited the final work. Finally, special thanks go to Catherine Moon for her patient and constructive critiques of the text. Cathy's support, encouragement, and painstaking assistance were instrumental to the writing of this book.

CONTENTS

ILLUSTRATIONS

THE ROLE OF METAPHOR
IN ART THERAPY

INTRODUCTION

I believe that all artworks are metaphoric depictions of the people who create them. In art therapy relationships, stories that unfold as artists create and interact with their artworks are not one-sided or exclusive conversations. Art therapists (along with the processes and products of art making, and people who make the art) are active partners of the dialogues. To illustrate the interaction, I share stories from the art therapy studio that describe an approach to art therapy focused on the central role of clients' metaphoric creations and art therapists' metaphoric responses.

The word metaphor is derived from the Greek *meta,* meaning above or beyond, and *phorein,* meaning to carry from one place to another (Kopp, R. R., 1995); the latter is the same root as *amphora,* an ancient Greek vessel for carrying and storing precious liquids. Metaphors in language are also carriers: They hold information that hides meaning in symbolic form. My book explores the functions, qualities, and characteristics of metaphors in art therapy, and examines methods of relating with and responding to metaphoric artworks and the artists who create them. I describe encounters with people from psychiatric hospitals and my private practice who literally and metaphorically wrestled with emotional problems and existential issues, and then discuss the role metaphors played in their therapeutic journeys.

Pragmatic and poetic, this book is a tribute to the complexities and mysteries of working with people who are suffering and striving to tell their stories through expressive artistic processes. Its roots lay deep in encounters with children, adolescents, and adults who have come to me for help over the last three decades. It is grounded in my interactions with graduate art therapy students and in my own encounters with important themes in life. I make no effort to affix particular meanings to the metaphors discussed in the clinical vignettes, but I do suggest ways to listen and respond to metaphoric communications.

Nearly every art therapist I know believes in the power of metaphoric imagery, and capacity of the creative process to unlock and deepen communication. Metaphoric imagery can provide clients and therapists psychological insights that go beyond linear rationality. However, there are significant differences in how art therapists behave toward and interact with the artworks people create.

Art therapists' theoretical and philosophical differences are evidenced in how they respond and relate to artworks, and the people who create them. For example, some art therapists emphasize the roles that art making and imagery play in facilitating verbal interaction in therapy. These art therapists believe that artworks and images are tools that assist in verbal psychotherapy. Other art therapists focus on the role of images as an indicator of dysfunction. These art therapists view artworks and images as projective aids in diagnosis. Still others regard art making as a practice of creating personal metaphors. From this perspective, art therapists act as beholders of, guides to, or creative assistants in the unfolding process, but the most important therapeutic agents are still the metaphors and clients who give the metaphors tangible form. Note that no single perspective is consistently superior; thus, many art therapists integrate a variety of approaches in their work, based on clients' unique needs.

In the methodology described in this book, art therapists do not necessarily seek to understand or interpret one single meaning of a client's artwork, but rather become advocates for a multitude of meanings. Although artworks are often mysterious and perplexing, they hold multiple truths that are open to many valid interpretations. As opposed to with systematic labeling or reductive interpretation of metaphoric messages, I approach clients' artworks with a sense of awe and wonder, and try to establish a respectful conversation with them that honors many possible meanings. In response to clients' metaphors, I often create stories or poems about the images, and encourage clients to do the same.

In art therapy sessions, I engage in dialogues with clients and their artworks in an effort to invite both to share stories. I often encounter art pieces that are disturbing, puzzling, and hard to grasp. Still, in nearly every circumstance, when I stay patient and keep an open mind, artworks inevitably uncover important meanings that are relevant to their creators. This book describes how to look at, listen to, and respond to the metaphors that artworks divulge.

"I am going to tell you a story." For as long as I can remember, these words have filled me with eagerness and excitement. As a child, the words meant that my mother was going to make some special time to read me a book. In elementary school, when the teacher announced story time, I celebrated the precious break from math and geography, which I perceived as inflexible and dull. Story time would set my imagination free. In church, whenever the minister said, "Let me tell you a story," I was lured from my daydreams into the heart of the homily. It didn't matter what the story was about, or even how poignant, funny, or profound it was. There was always something immediate that captured my imagination and caused me to almost forget to breathe until the story ended.

Today, stories continue to capture my imagination. Some of my favorite stories are parables, a word derived from the Greek *para-bole,* meaning juxtaposition for the sake of comparison (Jones, 1969). In its simplest form, the parable conveys a single message by juxtaposing an abstract demand, and a vivid story or situation. Parables have both literal and figurative meanings, which listeners typically interpret themselves.

As an art therapist, I regard clients' metaphoric artworks as being akin to parables. There is a juxtaposition of the physical objects people create and the life experiences they bring to the moment of creation. My therapeutic goal is to help people explore different interpretations of their art so they themselves can decide what it means. To do this, I avoid making overt my preferred interpretations of their artworks. If I assign a particular meaning to a client's creation, I undermine the client's own ability to discover meaning. On the other hand, when the meaning of a client's art piece remains implicit, the interpretive work is left for the client. For art therapists, the ability to wait for clients to make their own interpretations invites a deeper therapeutic relationship.

Clients often interpret their works different from how I would. Sometimes this is difficult for me because I want my clients to understand my point and learn from my experiences. But I recognize that in poking around for themselves in metaphors, clients often come up with understandings that are truer, deeper, and more personally significant than anything I could have said. What people realize on their own from metaphors becomes truths they can harvest for themselves—

not merely my truth, which they can passively accept or actively reject.

S. B. Kopp (1976) suggests three basic ways to know: through rational thought, empirical observation, and metaphor. "We can know things *rationally,* by thinking about them. If they seem logically consistent within themselves and with what else we know, we accept them as being true" (p. 21); this way of knowing is perhaps the most familiar mode. Another way of knowing is through empirical observation. "In this case we depend upon our senses, truth being a matter of perceiving correctly" (p. 21). A third way of knowing is through metaphor:

> In this mode we do not depend primarily on thinking logically nor on checking out our perceptions. Understanding the world metaphorically means we depend on an intuitive grasp of situations, in which we are open to the symbolic dimensions of experience. (p. 21)

What S. B. Kopp describes as metaphorical knowing is related to Allen's (1995) idea that art is a way of knowing. Allen suggests that imagination is a resource through which one can perceive life's possibilities and options. "Art making is a way to explore our imagination and to begin to allow it to be more flexible, to learn how to see more options" (p. 4). When people explore the world metaphorically through art making, they gradually learn to rely on their intuitive understandings of situations and experiences, and open themselves to multiple meanings that coexist.

In the following chapters, I share vignettes to illustrate different roles metaphors play in art therapy and describe ways that art therapists can creatively interact with clients and their artworks. Ultimately, this book is an expression of faith in the central role of metaphoric art making and metaphoric responses to artworks created in art therapy contexts. I trust in the inherent healing power of art and metaphoric understandings, and I hope this work affirms this same faith in other art therapists. The ideas presented in this text call for commitment to methods that immerse art therapists and clients in metaphors, mysteries, and the unpredictable processes of artistic creation.

BRUCE L. MOON
Mundelein, IL. 2007

Chapter I

METAPHOR AND INDIRECT COMMUNICATION IN THERAPY

The Pilot Who Would Be a Teacher[1]

Once upon a time, not all that long ago, in a land untouched by modernity, unspoiled by television, undamaged by fossil fuel emissions, and unharmed by the ravages of global corporations, the inhabitants of a certain village awoke to find that during the night, a large silver bird had come to rest in the clearing. The leader of the tribe sent word to all the huts, and soon after sunrise, the residents of the village gathered at the edge of the meadow to watch (what they presumed to be) God sleeping.

When the airplane pilot roused from her slumber, she was taken aback as she peered out the cockpit window at row upon row of men, women, and children staring reverently at her machine.

The pilot cautiously opened the side hatch and walked out on a wing. The members of the tribe immediately fell to the ground, quivering and praying that the woman who emerged from the side of God would not harm them. The pilot was amused. She was, after all, a well-educated woman, and not particularly religious at that. She thought, "How quaint, but how foolish. I will teach these sadly uninformed people all about airplanes."[1]

The pilot raised her hands and beckoned the people. Hesitantly the villagers arose and approached her. When all had come closer, the pilot turned with a flourish and re-entered her craft. She engaged the engine, and with a dramatic roar, the propellers spun and lights flashed.

When she looked out the window, the pilot was irritated to see all the people laying face down in the dirt, covering their heads in supplication. She turned off the engine and went back out onto the wing, trying desperately to think of some way to

---

1. This story appears in a slightly altered form in *Existential art therapy: The canvas mirror* by B. L. Moon, 1990 and 1995.

teach them about the technology of airplanes. She began to speak, but at a silent signal from their leader, all the villagers raised their spears and threw. The pilot was killed instantly.

    The village residents erected a shrine on that very spot. Each year, on the anniversary of the pilot's death, they offer sacrifices to the silver bird in hopes that God will never again roar at them. So far this sacrificial ritual seems to have worked.

The pilot's response to the villagers' fears and lack of knowledge was to attempt to teach them, or at least tell them, the truth about airplanes. Alas, people seldom welcome truths they are not prepared to handle. Contrary to the saying, truth often does not set people free, and sadly, it does not necessarily change attitudes, beliefs, or biases. In this story, the modern, well-educated pilot didn't realize the awesome power of the metaphor she was. She also was operating from the mindset of a colonizer, not recognizing that her worldviews differed from those of the villagers. She assumed her perspective was the right one—the only one, in fact. She neglected to consider how the cultural beliefs and traditions of the villagers might impact their perspectives and misunderstandings. Failure to understand the power of metaphor, coupled with cultural imperialism, was a deadly combination for the pilot.

Nomenclature

The following are brief explanations of words and phrases I developed that are important to concepts presented in this text:

- Therapeutic metaphor—a story, parable, artwork, sound, movement, or other form of metaphoric image that is analogous to a situation in the client's life. When therapists use this indirect communication of a metaphor, clients may respond more openly to conversations that could have been met with more defensiveness. For example, a therapist working with a client with unhealthy defensive behavior might call attention to positive and negative consequences of it by describing a fieldstone wall around a garden that protects vegetables from animal predators and yet constricts sunlight needed for growth.
- Visual (image) metaphor—an artwork or artistic process through which one thing (the artist) is described in terms of another (the

image). In the broadest sense, all artworks are overt or covert descriptions of the artists who create them.

- Aural metaphor–an acoustic phenomenon in which one thing (the subject) is described in terms of another (the sound).
- Kinetic metaphor–a physical movement or gesture in which one thing (the subject) is described in terms of another (the action).
- Milieu metaphor–a physical setting that describes one thing (the subject) in terms of another (the environment).
- Metaphoretician–a term I devised (Moon, B. L., 1990, 1995) to describe one who skillfully and spontaneously uses metaphors to uncover and convey truths. A metaphoretician is inclined to speculative contemplation and action in response to metaphors.
- Metaverbal–a term I devised (Moon, B. L., 1990, 1995) to describe art therapy as a treatment modality that transcends words.

Advantages of Metaphors in Psychotherapy

Metaphors have been vital to communication among humans throughout history. From time immemorial, stories, parables, proverbs, fables, and fairy tales have been used to convey essential truths about the human condition. Found in the epic tale *Gilgamesh* and parables of Jesus, as well as contemporary novels, metaphors carry potent messages that help people create and discover meaning in their lives.

It is easy to understand why verbal are incorporated in psychotherapy. But before discussing the benefits of metaphors in art therapy, I explore how metaphors support traditional psychotherapy. Generally speaking in this section, I refer to metaphors generated by psychotherapists and describe advantages to conveying messages metaphorically rather than through more direct, literal, or confrontational means.

First, well-constructed metaphoric stories are interesting. Stories have the capacity to capture the listener's imagination and inspire new considerations of situations in unique ways. A second advantage is that metaphors present their messages indirectly, disguised by the images of the story. This indirect route allows for a subtler, less confrontational delivery of messages: The listener can simply respond to surface meanings of the story if they are implicit, or if deeper meanings are too threatening or discomforting. Third, metaphoric stories are effective because listeners can interpret stories their own ways, determining the points of metaphors themselves.

A fourth advantage is that metaphoric communication in psychotherapy makes clients responsible for the personal changes that are the goal of therapy because clients decide what metaphors mean. When therapists present their messages directly, as in the form of specific advice, clients may follow the advice. If this advice leads to unsatisfactory results, clients may blame therapists; conversely, if therapists' advice leads to positive outcomes, clients may attribute success to therapists rather than to their own hard work.

A fifth advantage of metaphoric communication is that it can be enjoyable for both clients and therapists. Communicating in this way may conjure up memories of other occurrences of storytelling that have pleasant associations for both clients and therapists. Barker (1985) suggests that telling stories often strengthens therapeutic relationships.

In summary, verbal metaphors in therapy can engage, inspire, and influence clients. Metaphors present new ways of perceiving a situation or experience, and enable the therapist to avoid being overly confrontational or prescriptive. Metaphoric stories are often ambiguous and indirect, holding potential for multiple interpretations. By virtue of these attributes, metaphors may help therapists develop positive therapeutic alliances by avoiding negative reactions to more overt confrontations.

Advantages of Metaphors in Art Therapy

Art therapy is a metaverbal approach to therapy. True, verbal metaphors are frequently used by art therapists; but it is important to understand that visual images (e.g., drawings, paintings, and sculptures) are also metaphoric, and that there are techniques that art therapists can use to respond to clients' metaphoric images. I consider all artworks created in the context of art therapy to be metaphoric of their creator; thus, the metaphors that receive the most attention in this text are those that emerge through the client's art-making process. There are many advantages to using visual, aural, kinetic, and milieu metaphors in art therapy, including:

1. Visual artworks are, by nature, stimulating. They have the capacity to liberate the imaginations of the creator and viewer alike, and may encourage insights that are inaccessible through linear discourse alone.

2. Artistic metaphors are indirect expressions and, therefore, less confrontational and psychologically threatening than direct statements. An artwork is an externalized object once removed from the artist who created it; this distance, if maintained by the therapist's response to it, establishes an element of safety for the client. Consider the difference between asking a client to "explain why you are defensive" and asking the same client to "draw walls." The content of the client's expressions might be similar in both instances, but the affective experience could be markedly different. The act of drawing a wall can be a safer, less anxiety-provoking way to deal with personal defenses. This quality of safety depends upon both the art therapist's ability to keep within the structure of the metaphor and the client's capacity to trust the art-making process.

3. When clients create an art piece, they gain access to the many layers of meaning contained in the metaphor at both conscious and unconscious levels. Even when a drawing appears to be a straight-forward or concrete expression of an idea, there may be processes the artist is consciously unaware of that are important. I observed an example of this when a client drew a picture of his favorite fairytale, *Jack and the Beanstalk*. At one level, the drawing was a simple depiction of Jack stealing the giant's precious golden egg. After exploring different meanings for the drawing, the client realized that at a deeper level, the drawing portrayed his lifelong struggle for recognition and acceptance from his aloof and overbearing father.

4. Artistic metaphors provide opportunities for clients to reframe their experiences by looking at situations from new perspectives and making them concrete in visual images. One client drew herself as a small mouse about to be stepped on by a large woman. The client's initial interpretation of the drawing was related to feelings she had about her older sister who, she said, "always put me down." Clearly, the client identified with the position of the mouse in the drawing. While those feelings were valid, the art therapist encouraged her to imagine herself in the position of the

woman. By doing this, the client was, for the first time, able to get in touch with the irrational fear the woman felt toward the tiny mouse. Reframing allowed the client to feel empathy for her sister, and that opened new channels of communication between them that eventually led to a more fulfilling relationship.

5. Artworks provide a "third member" in therapeutic relationships. In art therapy, the client, art therapist, and artwork are equal partners. The client and art therapist can each create an artwork to express thoughts and feelings that otherwise might be regarded as unacceptable or difficult to articulate in words. I have seen this dynamic many times in encounters with children. Several years ago, I worked with a little girl whose mother was struggling with alcoholism. The girl was shy and soft-spoken, and whenever she was asked directly about her relationship with her mother, she always responded that everything was fine. One day, she drew a picture of a little boy and woman throwing stones at each other. As she looked at the picture, she said, "The little boy is very angry and hurt, and that is why he is throwing stones at his mommy."

6. The activities of making and sharing visual metaphors promote rapport between the art therapist and client. When an art therapist creates art alongside the client, the act of working together encourages a relationship that goes deeper than words. Likewise, when an art therapist observes the client making art, a sense of shared experience may foster relationship formation. Sharing stories connected with artworks can be pleasurable. Information is exchanged between the client and art therapist that is often perceived as non-threatening and enjoyable.

7. When art therapists communicate with clients through their own visual metaphors, they create opportunities to support, inform, engage, offer interpretations, provoke thought, and gently confront clients in safe, psychologically non-threatening ways.

Metaphor: Therapeutic Sense or Nonsense

Despite the advantages of using metaphors in both verbal and art therapy, metaphoric communication has its detractors. Some believe the indirect nature of metaphors is not conducive to efficient, time-limited therapy. The benefits of metaphoric openness and potential for multiple interpretations are also debatable. Therapists who prefer a more prescriptive approach to therapy, in which a client's problem is identified and the therapist intervenes to resolve the client's problem, may view the use of metaphors as unpredictable and vague. Also, some clients come to therapy looking for pragmatic solutions to problems, not insight or deeper understandings of their inner lives.

Note that depth psychology approaches have limitations, particularly for art therapists working in clinical settings that serve clients from a variety of cultural backgrounds. For some clients, an open-ended, depth approach may be irrelevant or even unhelpful.

R. R. Kopp (1995) traces such divergent views of the therapeutic use of metaphor to the contrasting philosophic perspectives of Aristotle and the positivists. Aristotle argues that the use of metaphor is a sign of genius in the poet. The capacity to make metaphors evidences an ability to see similarities in dissimilar subjects, and reframe these similarities in mental pictures that convey meanings. From Aristotle's perspective, metaphors are sensible.

Philosophers in the positivist tradition, however, emphasize objectivity, fact, and logic, and maintain that metaphors are frivolous and nonessential at best, if not outright dangerous and "logically perverse" (Kopp, R. R., 1995, p. 92). The positivist objection to metaphors is related to the lack of literal truth. For example, describing a person as having a head of granite is intended to convey qualities of stubbornness and inflexibility through metaphor, but is not a literal statement. For the positivist, truth is confined to the realm of either-or factual and linear logic in which similarity and difference cannot coexist. In this tradition, metaphors are nonsense.

A Poetic Digression

These divergent philosophic views of metaphor are in some ways analogous to the position of the art therapy profession in relation to health care insurance companies. Some third-party payers view art therapy as a significant treatment modality capable of helping clients in profound ways; these payers are willing to reimburse art therapists for their services. Other health insurance companies refuse to cover art therapy services because they view the discipline as ancillary and nonessential. Several years ago, I wrote the following poem to express feelings I had about managed care companies and the commercialization of health care in the United States:

Burning Lamentation

The CEO of the HMO
tried to steal my heart
with energy and synergy
he tried to tear my chest apart
length-of-stay cut down to three days
he said my life's work is a frill
I was downsized and ostracized
he circled in for the kill

The CEO of the HMO
tried to steal my heart
with deft precision he made his incision
his hands wrapped tight
he pulled, I felt his grip
he pulled, I heard it rip
but sure as hell
I lived to tell
he left a hole but
could not amputate my soul

Nietzsche said God is dead
God said Neitzsche is dead
CEO said you are dead
I said, this too shall pass
      this too shall pass

–From *The gate is not burning*, by B. L. Moon, 1997

SUMMARY

Throughout history, metaphors have been important in our effort to convey information and foster a sense of mutual understanding and empathy. Fundamental truths about the human condition have always been expressed metaphorically in stories, parables, and fables. In art therapy, visual metaphors offer many advantages. Artworks stimulate imagination and encourage insight that may be unreachable through talking. Indirect expressions, artworks may be psychologically less threatening than direct statements. Artistic processes and products access many layers of meaning, both conscious and unconscious. Artistic metaphors help clients reframe their experiences by looking at situations from new perspectives and making them concrete in visual images. Artworks provide a "third member" in therapeutic relationships. In art therapy, the client, art therapist, and artwork are equal partners in the relationship. The client and art therapist can each create an artwork to express thoughts and feelings that otherwise might be regarded as unacceptable or difficult to articulate in words. Visual metaphors foster opportunities to support, inform, engage, offer interpretations, provoke thought, and gently confront clients in ways that are potentially safe and psychologically non-threatening.

Chapter II

THE ART THERAPIST
AS METAPHORETICIAN

Metaphoretician—one who skillfully and spontaneously uses visual,
aural, and kinetic metaphors to uncover and convey truths.

THE STORY OF *IT*

As a child, I remember hearing about *it* often. I was not sure what *it* was and the grown-up world seemed unwilling to share *it* with me.

I knew that my father hadn't made *it*. I knew that my mother often cried about *it*. I knew that *it* made my older sister angry. And I knew that strangers would sometimes sigh, shake their heads, and say, "Isn't *it* a shame." The only thing I didn't know was what *it* was.

When I asked my mother, "What is *it*?" she would stop whatever she was doing and say, "It's better that you don't know."

When I asked my friends about *it*, they laughed and said, "*It* doesn't matter."

I asked many people to define *it* and received many partial explanations, but no one ever told me precisely what *it* was. I knew, without knowing why, that *it* was important. So I asked everyone who I thought should know, "What is the meaning of *it*?" But if they knew what *it* was, they weren't telling me. Now, many years later, I know that they were not intentionally deceiving me or keeping the meaning of *it* secret; the truth was (and is) that they simply didn't know any more about *it* than I did.

Clients have often entered my studio bearing the unspoken question, "What is the meaning of *it*?" Their individual *it* has been feelings:

Figure 2. Looking for *It*.

a sadness they could not explain, an anger that boiled within, or a secret hurt kept buried. The children, adolescents, and adults who have sought my help over the last 30 years have longed for me to help them figure out what *it* means. Many clients I have worked with, whether in my private practice or in the psychiatric hospital, suffered the anguish of knowing that their lives were painful, dysfunctional, and traumatic. They came bearing histories of neglect, abuse, or confusion in hopes that they would be understood and that they would come to new understandings of their life stories. Typically, they had already tried to express their truths to therapists from other disciplines, but had not been able convey the crucial themes of their lives in words. As an art therapist, my job is to look at, listen to, interact with, and respond to metaphoric stories that clients portray through the images they make. I am, for all intents and purposes, a *metaphoretician.*

In literature, a metaphor is a word, phrase, or expression used in a figurative way to compare two seemingly unrelated subjects. In linguistic metaphors, an object is described as being a second object. Metaphoric description suggests that the first object has some of the qualities of the second. In this way, the first object can be efficiently and powerfully described because implicit and explicit attributes from the second object can be used to enhance the description of the first. People often confuse metaphors and similes. The difference is that metaphors (which are, not are like) create transformations that protect clients and give them perspective from a distance instead of just comparing for straight understanding. The economic quality of metaphoric description is often exploited in prose and poetry, in which few words, emotions, and meanings from one context are poignantly transferred to a different subject. Art therapists go beyond the verbal limitations of these literary understandings of metaphor by interacting with the metaphors found in visual images, sounds, and movements.

When people create art, they are working with, playing with, and enacting important life themes. A critical task for art therapists is to grasp and respond to truths that emerge in the creation of visual metaphors. These metaphors are expressed through the symbolic actions of making and tangible art objects that result.

As people in art therapy make art, they are engaged in a process of transforming inner images into observable forms. By doing this, they translate truths of their lives into actions and visual objects. According to Arnheim (1966), "The metaphor, then, distills from reality-situations the deeper, underlying aspects of life, for whose sake alone art creates images of reality" (p. 279).

A Learning Exercise

Early in the fall semester of each new academic year, I work with first-year graduate students to help them understand the importance of metaphors in art therapy. I begin the class by holding up a worn, slightly deflated football. I toss the ball to one of the students, Kris, and ask, "What are you holding?"

Kris turns the football in her hands and says, "I am holding a flat football."

"Very good," I say. "But what does it mean to you?"

Examining it more, she says, "I don't know, I guess it reminds me of my brothers." She laughs and throws it back to me.

I toss the ball to another student, Marianne. "What are you holding?" I ask. "Oh, by the way, you can't repeat anything Kris said."

Marianne squeezes the ball and says, "I am holding Friday nights in high school: bonfires and pep rallies." She returns the ball to me.

"Excellent!" I say upon catching it. "You know, it reminds me of being part of the team, being part of something bigger than me."

I toss the ball again and ask, "Sean, what are you holding?"

Sean grimaces. "I am holding all the times I felt rejected and put down by the jocks at school," he says. "Man, I hated-still hate-football." He hands me the ball, which I lateral to Ali.

"What are you holding, Ali?" I ask.

"I was a cheerleader," she says, "so I am holding a lot of work and fun." She throws a nice spiral my direction.

I hand it off to Marla who says, "I am holding a ball that needs more air, more tension, and more pressure in order to do what it is intended to do."

I gently lob the ball to Renee. She smells the old leather, sighs, and says, "I am holding all that's left of a living thing."

I pass the football to Bill who says: "I am holding a symbol of my football coach from middle school. He was great. I think I would have tried to run through a wall if he asked me to. I love playing football."

The ball goes to Maria. "I am thinking about touch-football games we used to play on the green in college, and that reminds me of guys and beer," she says.

I hand the ball to Katie. "I think about how my dad used to fall asleep watching TV on Sunday afternoons," she says. "If I tried to change the channel, he'd get mad and say he was just resting his eyes."

The ball makes its way to every member of the class. Memories of tailgating and parties, disappointments and successes, being chosen first and last in gym class, and the earthy smells of fall are recounted. Each reaction to the football is unique. There are many reactions and many interpretations of the same object. As the exercise proceeds, students become aware of how different each person's reaction to the ball is, and there is a dawning awareness that differences are accounted for by the particular life experiences of each student.

After everyone in the class comments, I again hold up the football and say, "I am holding a metaphor." This simple exercise dramatically demonstrates an aspect of encountering metaphors. In this task, students bring the whole of their life experiences to the encounter with the football, and for each student, the memories stirred and emotions recalled are personal and unique. Imagine if I asked them to draw the football. Although everyone would be looking at the same object, many different images of the ball would be created, and each would hold particular stories and emotional associations.

It is the same when people create art, for they are making visible pieces of their own story, slivers of their reality. Artists show themselves to the world through representations, narratives, abstractions, and non-representations of the world. No single artwork is a complete portrait of the artist, but in a sense, every image an artist creates is at least a partial self-portrait, a.k.a. a metaphor of the artist's life.

For art therapists, there is some cause for caution regarding the idea that every image is a partial self-portrait of the person who created it. One concern is that art therapists may have difficulty seeing beyond their own interpretations of metaphors and, thus, get in the way of a client's expression. For instance, thinking of the students in the football exercise, imagine Ali as the therapist for Sean. Sean could draw a football and intend for it to be an expression of pain and anger, but Ali's positive associations to football might preclude her capacity to show empathy for Sean's expression.

Another concern is that one may be tempted to interpret images literally in search of meaning. I encountered an example of this in a discussion with a supervisee, Laurie, as we looked at an image of a tree that one of her clients created (Figure 3). Laurie was particularly inter-

Figure 3. Wounded Tree.

ested in the dark crevice in the trunk of the tree. She said, "My client seldom acknowledges her pain overtly, so I was really struck by this symbolic wound."

I responded, "You knew it was a wound?"

"Well, yes," she said. "When a real tree has a hole like that in the trunk, it is usually a sign of some trauma. Something happened that hurt the tree, and so I assume that when an image of a tree has a mark like this on it, it probably represents a trauma of some sort."

"You might be right, Laurie," I said. "Did you talk with your client about this part of the drawing?"

"Yes," she replied. "I asked her, what happened that hurt the tree?"

"And how did she respond?" I asked.

Laurie thought for a moment and then said: "She did not say much at all. Like I said earlier, she doesn't like to talk about her pain."

I said, "Your question was really an interpretation and intervention."

"What do you mean?" she asked.

"Well, by asking what happened that hurt the tree, you conveyed to the artist your interpretation that it was something painful," I explained. "You made your interpretation of the dark crevice apparent in how you worded your question."

"Is that wrong?" Laurie asked.

"Laurie, I am not saying you were wrong; you may well be on the right track regarding this image," I said. "The crevice may indicate some past trauma in the life of the client; but by making your interpretation literal—assuming that because a hole in a real tree is a sign of damage, the hole depicted in this drawing is also an indicator of some painful historic event—you limit the possibilities of the image. All I am suggesting is that there may be many possible meanings. Your selection of one literal meaning may have inadvertently restricted your interaction with your client."

"What are some other possibilities?" she asked.

I explained: "There are so many potential meanings for such an image. The crevice might be a symbolic opening: an opening to the self, a way out of the self, or something beyond the self. It might be a safe place for an animal to live. It might be a place of mystery. It might have been caused by a lightning strike. It might be the remnant of a woodsman's failed attempt to cut the tree down and, thereby, a symbol of survival. Some might say it appears to be vaginal, so it might symbolize feminine sexuality. It might be the last trace of a branch that is no longer part of the tree."

Laurie replied, "Some of those things you just said sound traumatic."

"Yes, I guess lightning striking or the woodsman's attempt to cut down the tree do sound that way; but the point is that all these and perhaps many more are possibilities, and only the artists themselves really know the meanings of the things they make," I said.

"Bruce, how would you have talked with her about the crevice?" Laurie asked.

"I think I would have said something like, 'I see a dark place near the base of the trunk,'" I said.

"That's it–that's all you would say?" Laurie asked. "What if she doesn't say anything?"

"Yes, Laurie, that's about it," I reaffirmed. "Or I might say something like, 'I wonder about the story of the tree, how that dark place was formed.' By making a simple open-ended statement, like 'I see a dark place,' I would invite the artist to go deeper into the story of her image. She would have the opportunity to share about her tree, or she might choose to say nothing, just as she did when you asked your interpretation-laden question. In either scenario, it is the artist-client who is in charge of interpreting the image, and ultimately that is the way it ought to be. In times of pain and confusion, when clients typically come to therapy, they are vulnerable to being steered in some direction even metaphorically and it is important for therapists to be cautious of overexerting our influence regarding already delicate issues. In court, the judge stops lawyers from leading witnesses, but in a counseling setting, it's up to you and this is an ethical choice."

"Earlier you said there were many possible interpretations of the crevice," Laurie said. "Are you saying now that only the artist's interpretation is important, and that you would never mention the other possibilities?"

No, not exactly," I replied. "If she responded to my saying that I see a dark place near the base of the tree by telling a story about how the crevice came into being, then I might respond by offering a different take on the story. But I would do so in the form of telling a story of my own, not by offering a specific interpretation of her image." Imagine this dialogue as an example:

Bruce: I see a dark place near the base of the tree.
Client: Yes, I'm not sure what happened there.
Bruce: It reminds me of a tree we had in our backyard when I was little. One day, there was a big storm and one of the tree's branches was blown off. It left a hole sort of like the one in your tree.

The client is free to consider my story, too. She might decide that my story also has meaning for her, or she might disregard it. The point is to be open-ended in the interaction, to offer comments about the image in such a way that she and I remain open to all possible meanings of the crevice in the trunk of the tree, rather than fix or direct its meaning. Or, to put it another way, sometimes it can be important for art therapists to have no point they are trying to make. The capacity of the therapist to wait for the client to find meanings makes the client responsible for personal growth and healing.

If, as Arnheim (1966) proposes, the purpose of metaphor is to expose deep underlying aspects of life, and if, as I state earlier, visual artworks are metaphoric representations of their creators, then the artworks created in art therapy contexts are powerful depictions of people's inner lives. As such, it is the responsibility of the client to interpret the meanings of artworks, and it is the mission of the art therapist to aid in the unearthing of meanings by acting as metaphoretician.

One of the most important roles of the art therapist is that of metaphoretician. Whether art therapists work in an inpatient or residential treatment facility, an outpatient clinic, a private practice, or some other setting, they should try to understand the metaphorical messages people send. These metaphoric communications are transmitted through dramatic and subtle actions, images, words, movements, sounds, and silences.

As metaphoreticians in residential treatment facilities, art therapists are often called upon to translate clients' metaphoric messages into theoretical understandings and treatment interventions appropriate to the therapeutic milieu. In an outpatient clinic, the art therapist may be called upon to explore the meanings of metaphoric dramas enacted in the clinical setting. In private practice settings, the success or failure of the therapeutic venture may depend upon the art therapist's capacity to relate to and appreciate the often mysterious and provocative metaphoric actions of the persons who come to them for help.

On the surface, interactions in art therapy seem similar to traditional verbal psychotherapeutic interactions. Although arts-based approaches and verbal approaches share some attributes, their fundamental differences are significant. Most notably, in chapters ahead, I illustrate understandings of and responses to metaphors that do not depend solely upon verbalization. I do not think that insights, growth, and therapeutic change can always be described in linear, discursive ways; rather, I agree with the old maxim, "A picture is worth a thousand words."

Prerequisites of the Metaphoretician

To be an effective metaphoretician, art therapists must strive to work creatively in therapy sessions. Each client requires unique responses and interventions. When a client shares problems, the art therapist must respond. After the session, the art therapist can retreat to the solitude of the office to reflect on the client's struggles and contemplate future interventions; but in face-to-face interactions with the person seeking help, the art therapist needs to respond immediately to achieve therapeutic effect.

Experienced art therapists do not rely on stock interventions. They do not think, "When the client complains of *this,* I will have him draw *that.*" Instead, they draw from their past experiences in order to look at, listen to, and respond to the client. They relate the client's struggles to their own experiences. They listen to the client's metaphoric language, which often belies underlying issues and conflicts the client cannot put into words. They take note of their own inner emotional reactions and share their thoughts in ways that express their own personalities and personal histories.

Art therapists often operate from a preferred theoretical orientation, but the actual flow of a given session is highly individualized and, thus, an improvisational art form. This is not to say that art therapists are unpredictable. On the contrary, predictability is a central element in the construction of psychological safety in therapeutic relationships, which I discuss more in Chapter IV. However, the ability to artistically improvise to adapt to the needs of each client, image, and session in a distinctive way distinguishes art therapists from technicians pre-programmed to respond to unpredictable situations in circumscribed ways.

The roots of the word *improvise* are found in Italian and French words meaning unprepared (Webster, 1988). Skilled artistic improvisers, however, know that authentic creative improvisation is built upon countless hours of disciplined preparation. A painter, musician, or art therapist, the improviser must be well educated in skills of the endeavor. Technical expertise promotes artistic self-expression and self-discovery. After attending graduate school in art therapy, novices typically need several years to acquire the tools and techniques to become masters of therapeutic and metaphoric improvisation.

Of course, technical competence alone does not ensure creative depth. Once the preferred theories and structures of the art therapy discipline have been mastered, the would-be metaphoric improviser must meet four psychological conditions (Phillips, 1988):

> (1) Have access to his past, (2) be able to focus his attention intensely on the present, (3) be comfortable giving up enough control over the outcome of his task to experiment as he performs, and (4) recognize the significance of accidental experience. (p. 184)

The first of these qualities, emotional access to the past, allows an art therapist to draw from an array of personal life experiences to generate ideas about, associations with, and metaphoric responses to a client's artworks. Pieces of the art therapist's past are reconfigured in unique new ways as the therapy process unfolds. Painters, musicians, and dancers develop distinctive artistic styles shown through a range of works with diverse content because of the interplay of their capacity for spontaneity and underlying artistic foundations. Likewise, art therapists also develop unique therapeutic styles based on the integration of their individual life experiences and theoretical orientation. As Phillips (1988) notes, "A therapist working with an adolescent patient, for instance, ought to have access to memories and feelings from his own adolescence" (p. 184). For art therapists, such memories are a wellspring of understanding that helps give form to unique metaphoric, therapeutic responses. Allowing fragments of past experience to become conscious exposes art therapists to the mystery of metaphoric responses to clients.

The second emotional prerequisite for the metaphoretician is the ability to focus on the present. An art therapist's associations to past events, as important as they are to metaphoric responsiveness, are only useful when they are connected to the present therapeutic interaction. The art therapist must be immersed in the phenomena of the present, focusing on the client's artworks and ideas, metaverbal messages, and sensory feedback. "With this kind of full and deep participation in the proverbial 'here and now,' the merger of one's immediate task and one's history begins to yield the process we recognize as creativity" (Phillips, 1988, p. 185).

The third psychological attribute required of the improvisational art therapist is the ability to surrender control of a task to allow for experimentation. As noted earlier, art therapists spend years learning to master therapeutic techniques. Paradoxically, this preparation allows art therapists to give up enough overt control to allow artistic improvisation and metaphoric responsiveness to occur. When art therapists let themselves to be led into the mysteries of the artworks and struggles of each new person who seeks their help, a quality of spontaneity and therapeutic excitement is created. Without this kind of openness to adventure, the work of art therapists becomes rote and emotionally detached.

Last, art therapists endeavor to be comfortable with the possibilities of accidental experience. Metaphoric and artistic responses are acts of improvisation formed in the interplay of mastery, past experience, concentration in the present, willingness to experiment, and openness to the accidental. Ideally, a lively balance between technique and spontaneity is struck. If art therapists work only from a set of prescribed techniques, competence may result, but seldom does creativity or inspiration. Likewise, if art therapists respond to people seeking help by only drawing from their own past reservoir of reactions, they may not be harmful, but they may not be helpful either. If art therapists rely only on the phenomena of the present, they may be flexible and spontaneous, but may also be disorganized and confusing. But if art therapists stir all that they have lived through into all that they are doing now, and if they blend technical mastery with a willingness to explore and healthy regard for things they cannot control, their work with metaphoric imagery will be dynamic and effective.

The Story of Mandy

What I knew about Mandy before I met her was that she was 16 years old, depressed, and recovering from an overdose of sleeping pills. She was admitted to the adolescent unit at the psychiatric hospital after a brief stay in a general hospital. However, prior to our first meeting, no written report could tell me how insufficient the word *depression* was. Mandy was sad: heartbreakingly sad. She was frightened, too, so fearful that she shuddered as she came into the studio. A tight inhalation accompanied her quickly averted eyes. There was a heartrending silence between us that seemed to say, "Please don't be mean to me."

My natural interactive style is outgoing and sociable, and sometimes a bit effusive, but I suspected this would be unacceptable in Mandy's presence. As I looked at her, the image of a deer in headlights flashed in my imagination, and I sensed that my usual exuberance would be construed as an assault by Mandy. Many things went through my mind. I recalled a time that my family went to a circus when I was little. I remembered walking between two tents where the elephants were grazing on bales of hay. One of the elephants rocked back and forth, straining the tether that held him in place. I felt small and afraid, and I cried. Someone picked me up and put me on his shoulders, and I knew I was safe. This scrap of memory filtered into my awareness of the present moment with Mandy.

Gently I said: "Mandy, my name is Bruce. They tell me that you like to draw and I do, too." I began to hang sheets of paper on the wall and took boxes of chalk out of the cupboard. I taped 3′ x 3′ brown kraft paper side-by-side.

Mandy said, "I think I'd better go back to my room."

I replied, "If that's what you want to do, Mandy, but it might be good to try to do some artwork."

She turned away from me and went to the door of the studio where the attendant was waiting outside. I watched as they walked across the hospital grounds toward the adolescent unit. Mandy looked fragile and frightened. I imagined the gray winter wind cutting into her. I felt a deep sadness, as the images of elephants from my childhood and a deer the headlights collided in my mind. It seemed to me that no one had been able to pick up Mandy and make her feel safe. I wondered if she viewed me as another predator in her world.

The next session went much like the first, with Mandy choosing to return to the adolescent unit rather than make art in the studio. As I taped paper to the wall at the beginning of the third session, Mandy opened the cabinet and gathered boxes of chalk. I noted this new behavior but chose not to comment on it. Instead I asked, "What would you like to draw?"

Mandy said, "I want to draw my tree."

In an effort to foster a relationship with her through shared activity, I asked, "Would it be okay if I draw a tree, too?"

Mandy shyly replied, "Sure, that would be good." The pastel chalks that Mandy selected were an inch in diameter, and we drew in silence for nearly an hour. I watched as Mandy pressed her chalk so hard against the wall that the brown crumbled in her hand. Sweat slid down her forehead.

As the end of the session neared, and she seemed to pause in her drawing, I asked, "Do you feel like talking about the drawing, Mandy?"

"No, not now," she said. "Can you save it though? Maybe we can talk about it another time."

"Sure," I said. "I'll save yours and mine, too."

She began to put the chalk away and said, "I think I'd like to go back now."

I looked at the door and said, "That's fine, Mandy, but I think the attendant has already left. Would it be okay if I walk you back to the unit?"

She gave me the trace of a smile and said, "That would be okay."

It was late afternoon and the snow fell softly around us. Mandy is as quiet as the snow, I thought. She held her coat tightly against her body, and seemed to fade within the down and nylon skin. Later, after I left her at the cottage and was making my way back to the art therapy studio, Bob Dylan's (1966) mournful song *Sad Eyed Lady of the Lowlands* played in my imagination as I thought about Mandy's vulnerability and sadness.

When Mandy entered the studio for our next session, she asked to work on her drawing of the tree again. I unrolled our papers and taped them to the wall. Mandy's drawing was of a forest, but one tree in the foreground stood out from the rest. Its roots lay exposed above the ground and its trunk had an ochre tint. In the middle of the trunk, there was a large blackened, hollowed-out place. She and I worked for another half-hour on our drawings. Mandy added more trees to the background, drew individual leaves, and filled in the empty places on her page with a myriad of tiny details.

Mandy stepped away from her drawing and said, "I think I am finished."

I suggested that we sit down and spend a few moments looking at each other's drawings. As a general rule, I encourage clients to tell me about their drawings before I talk about mine, but because Mandy was so reticent to talk about her work, I decided to describe my drawing first. I pointed to it and said: "This tree stands in the middle of a wheat field. It's been here a long time. There is a farm a long way off on the edge of the field, but for now the tree is by itself" (Figure 4).

Mandy asked, "What kind of tree is it?"

"An oak, I think," I said. "Its roots go deep into the ground."

Figure 4. Lone Tree.

She asked, "Why is it so gnarly?"

I thought for a moment and then said: "The tree has had its share of stormy times. I guess that made it grow funny."

Mandy said, "It looks lonely."

"It is, sometimes," I said. "But there is a farmer who comes out and eats his lunch there in the shade. And kids come and play on the low branches."

Mandy glanced at me and said: "That sounds nice. My tree isn't like that at all."

I looked at her drawing and said, "The drawing looks dark."

"Yeah, it's scary in there," she added. Mandy went on to tell me her forest was too thick to walk through. Then she focused on the tree with the gaping hole. "Wouldn't this one be pretty if it were in a park?"

"Yes," I said. "It's a great tree. It looks strong."

"It used to be even stronger," she said. "Somebody has been taking the dirt away." She pointed to where the roots lay above the ground.

"I wonder why," I said.

"Me, too," she agreed.

I said, "That is a mean thing to do to a tree."

Mandy replied, "Mean things happen in here."

I leaned closer to the paper to get a better look and said, "That hole in the trunk looks like it might have hurt."

Mandy did not respond, so I tried another approach. "Sometimes squirrels build nests in places like that," I said.

Mandy turned away and said, "I don't think anything could live in there."

I asked, "Could you pretend to go in there for awhile and look around?"

"No, I don't want to," she said.

"No?" I asked.

"Bruce, I'd be too scared to be in there," she said.

"I'll go in with you if you want," I offered.

She replied, "But it's so dark."

For a moment I felt stuck, unsure of what to do or say in response. I decided to take another therapeutic risk: Improvise. I stood and asked, "Can I draw on your page?" She nodded.

In her dark, hollow place, I drew a kerosene lantern with a bright yellow light (Figure 5). I stepped away from the drawing, turned toward her, and said: "Now we have a light. Can you draw what you might see in this place?"

Mandy stood up and drew a broken golden ring, liquor bottle, and ticket to an amusement park. When she finished, tears trickled down her cheeks. She asked, "Can we talk about this next time?"

I said: "If you want to talk next session, that's fine, but I think I understand already. It seems like it must hurt to look at these things." I approached her drawing with a dark chalk in my hand.

"Maybe I should turn out the light," I said, moving as if to draw over the yellow light but hoping she would stop me.

"No," she said. "Leave it alone. It's okay to look at that stuff." With that, she went into the next room to wash her hands.

In months that followed, light became a recurring metaphoric theme in our sessions. Sometimes the light was in the form of a torch, other times a flashlight, and occasionally a spotlight. Mandy, in her quiet and hesitant way, slowly allowed herself to bring more things into the light. Scenes of abuse from an alcoholic father were illuminated. Memories of the battles between her parents prior to and during their separation and divorce were made visible. The spotlight cast

Figure 5. Mandy's Tree.

by her drawings revealed a tragic drama of disappointment and loss. With each session, Mandy became more comfortable, less frightened. Through her art, she began to allow herself to see and claim feelings and thoughts she had tucked away deep in her own dark forest. As she shared them in the community of two that our sessions comprised, she experienced the satisfaction of being understood by someone else.

In this vignette, my emotional access to the past was evident in the first encounter with Mandy, as the memory of my experience with the elephant filtered into my awareness of Mandy in the present. My capacity to focus attention on the "here and now" with Mandy made me sensitive to the need to tone down my typical relating style and guided me in my interactions with her. In early stages of our relationship, my attention to the present resulted in giving Mandy permission to return to her cottage almost as soon as she arrived for therapy. I learned to accept that I could not control whether she stayed in the studio long enough to make art. I learned to tolerate my own anxiety about Mandy's participation and give up my desire to be in control of our therapy sessions. This relinquishing of control freed me to talk about my tree as a way to encourage Mandy to share her feelings about her drawing. The interaction with Mandy on the day I asked if I could draw on her page was, in many ways, a therapeutic improvisation; I had not planned to engage with her in that manner. Nevertheless, that experience has forever made me sensitive to the importance of improvisational encounters.

One key to metaphoric interaction in art therapy is the art therapist's ability to access many aspects of self–memories, techniques, therapeutic skills, and creative hunches–in service of the therapy. Therapeutic metaphors are all around, all the time. They come in fragments of memory. They come in associations to the life circumstances of those who seek help. Elders of our discipline hand them down, and they are thrust upon us by our clients' artworks. As art therapists, we must open ourselves to the process of metaphoric improvisation to creatively and authentically interact with our clients and their images.

Summary

Metaphors are important to the art therapy discipline. They enable us to understand and respond to the experiences of our clients, and help us explore meanings in our clients' and our own artworks. The great value of visual metaphorical thinking is that new light is shed on clients' lives through the phenomena of their own art making, and clients' artworks serve as creative instruments of self-expression and self-discovery.

Chapter III

THE METAPHOR OF THE
THERAPEUTIC JOURNEY

In geometry, we learn that the shortest distance between two points is a straight line. In art therapy, however, if entry into the therapy relationship marks one point, and termination of therapy another, the path between them is seldom straight. More often, the expanse between these two points is marked by twisting turns, dead ends, and poorly tended trails that descend into dark crevices; in other words, there is no easy passage. The metaphoric image that often describes therapy is a journey or pilgrimage. Throughout history, people have set out on such journeys, on spiritual quests and personal pilgrimages. "Driven by pain, drawn by longing, lifted by hope, singly and in groups, they come in search of relief, enlightenment, peace, power, joy or they know not what" (Kopp, S. B., 1972, p. 3).

Art therapy journeys are undertaken for many reasons. Some clients begin out of despair, some out of anxiety or crisis, and some out of a deep belief that somehow their lives could be, should be, better. Some people are forced into the early steps of the journey by authority figures or significant others in their lives who are concerned that something is wrong with the person's current path.

Who are these clients who undertake the art therapy journey? What brings them to our studios, offices, hospitals, schools, and treatment programs? In over 30 years of art therapy practice, I have yet to encounter anyone who comes to me happy and having a great time in life. Rather, people come out of pain, turmoil, emotional chaos, and fear. They come bearing inner scars from histories of physical and emotional abuse, neglect, physical challenges, and disenfranchisement. Each person carries personal stories that are often painful, scary, hurtful, or horrific.

Given this reality, people often begin the art therapy journey wanting change, but secretly hoping for the art therapist to comfort them without their having to undergo the difficult process of psychic and behavioral change. It is as if they enter the studio saying, "My life is a mess, and you have to clean it up."

An initial goal in the face of this unspoken demand is to help clients become immersed in the metaphor of the therapeutic journey. This goal is often challenging for me because I, too, harbor inner wishes to clean up messy situations. I consider myself helpful and wise from experience, and am tempted to pretend that I am powerful enough to provide solutions to all the clients' problems; however, I realize that my solutions to problems would be of little or no help to clients. It is as if the client stands holding an invisible lasso at the door of the studio. I welcome the client who in turn hurls the rope, attempting to ensnare me so I can make everything better. I step away to elude the noose, and the rope falls limp to the floor. The client is taken aback and disappointed by my evasion. It is a dance, and I must move in such a way as to avoid the noose, and yet encourage and welcome the client into the therapeutic endeavor. If I am adequately skilled in this therapeutic dance of evasion, and if the client is brave and determined enough, the client may transform this desire to be taken care of into curiosity about oneself, learning to use imagination to discover ways to resolve struggles.

The client sometimes begins with the hope that the art therapist will offer something permanent, some unchanging course of action upon which to depend. Instead, the art therapist offers immersion in imagination, and explorations in flowing color and impermanent chalk marks: reflections on the way life is an evolving, ambiguous, and mysterious epic narrative. Whatever brings the person to the therapeutic quest, be it a search for peace, understanding, love, joy, or meaning, is a metaphoric journey into life that can restore and enliven the traveler's existence. The creation of images offers people new perspectives on the meanings of their lives. Art therapists communicate through metaphor and image, but clients change and heal through the creation and sharing of personal artworks and stories. Each client's unique self is an evolving composite of cultural myths, mores, and narratives, mixed with the individual's personal chronicle.

But what of the persons who cannot, or will not, tell their tales? This is where the making of art comes in. For many years, I worked with children, adolescents, and adults who were physically or sexually abused, or both. They came to the therapeutic arts studio at the hospital because their feelings affected their behavior, causing them to act out, harm themselves, distrust others, be aggressive, or feel miserable. Yet as uncomfortable and disturbing as their feelings and behaviors were, they could not, or would not, speak of what they endured. Children literally had no words, no vocabulary to adequately describe what happened to them and how they felt about it. Adolescents often were so angry at the adult world that the last thing they wanted to do was talk with an adult about their lives. Adults lamented about being at a loss for words.

For these people and many others, the art therapy process is an adventure in visual narration. In the early stages of the process, the client must visually tell a tale, and the art therapist must introduce the idea that the creation of artworks produces guidance. The creation of images that serve as metaphors of the artist activates a process of transformation from a person held captive and victimized by the past, to one who is the creator of the story.

As creator of one's own story, the client is in charge, having the capacity to accept, paint over, rework, or completely alter the artwork. While the creation of images is a good start, it is not enough. As the therapeutic journey unfolds, clients portray stories. As clients paint, draw, or sculpt tales, someone must see, hear, and try to understand their images.

When I am in the studio working with clients, I not only look at and listen to their stories, but I also portray mine for them to see. If we are to gain anything from this shared pilgrimage, we need to get to know each other. I usually make art as I accompany others in their journeys. The mutual exchange of images fosters reciprocal self-disclosure, and such discoveries often lead to the sharing of vulnerabilities, both the clients' and mine. In the metaphor of the therapeutic pilgrimage, I, too, am a traveler. As an art therapist, I know interesting ways to look at the road signs, the images my companions make, but I am not a tour guide or highway patrolman limiting speed or directing the flow of traffic; on the contrary, we are in this together, a design that helps me remain faithful to the painting and repainting of my tale. This helps me stay honest with myself. To really encourage travelers to become open with me, I must begin by being open to myself.

As I work on my own art, I continually unveil my inner life. I cannot help but bump against feelings and thoughts that are unpleasant, discomforting, and malevolent if I am also to hold the tender, warm, and respectable aspects of who I am. These strong/weak, virtuous/vile, profane/sacred images must be painted and seen for me to be able to be with the images of my fellow travelers. My resolution to be open to my own images is an unending struggle, and I hope that this encourages a similar commitment in the people with whom I work. Their courage, often in the face of intensely painful histories, contributes to my ability to be courageous and open to myself. Again, there is a principle of spiraling reciprocity at work: Their courage inspires my courage, my courage inspires their images, and their images inspire my courage, all of which inspires more images, and so on and so forth. Of course, in therapy context, visual narratives of the struggling person should always receive priority. I am not implying that my images are the focus of the journey; however, they do become elements of the landscape the client and I traverse. Sometimes my paintings provide subtle background; other times, they help point others toward a possible direction. Still other times, my images recede beyond the horizon. By creating and sharing artworks, I get to know struggling people, and they get to know me.

Thus far, I describe how clients and I draw pictures, make paintings, and write poems about our lives. In the vignette that follows, I explain how I sometimes respond to clients' artworks through movement and sound. Their stories move me, and sometimes mine move them. Together, we embark on a therapeutic and artistic pilgrimage.

The Path that Brought You Here

To introduce the metaphoric theme of art therapy as a journey, I often ask people to create an image of the path that has brought them to therapy. The following vignette is a snapshot of the early stages of the journey. Following the vignette, I discuss metaphoric aspects of the interaction and therapeutic implications of the session.

Emma

Emma was referred to my private practice. She came with the complaint that she often felt empty and "uncomfortably numb." She was a pleasant woman in her mid-20s who seemed shy. "Welcome to the studio, Emma," I said when we met.

She made only hesitant eye contact with me as she told me she had been in therapy with a counselor for several months when she was an adolescent. She said, "He was nice and everything, and I think it helped to talk to him, but it's been awhile, and now I just can't shake this feeling that there is something missing."

Emma told me she worked in a department store, was attending college part-time, and wanted to become an elementary school teacher.

"What would you like to get out of art therapy?" I asked.

"I'm not really sure," she replied. "A friend of mine is studying to become an art therapist, and she seems to think it might help me, so I thought, why not try it?"

I asked again, "Do you have any idea what you want from our relationship?"

She thought for a moment, glanced at me, and said, "I want to really feel again–you know, feel like I am alive."

"Well, let's get started," I said. I showed her around the studio, orienting her to where the art supplies were kept. "Okay, now that you have gotten a feel for the options here, what media would you like to use for your first task?" I asked. She selected a large sheet of brown kraft paper and box of chalk. "Emma, I'd like you to draw the path that has brought you here," I said.

She looked puzzled. "I'm not sure how to start," she said. "I haven't really done artwork since high school."

I replied: "Don't worry about it, Emma. I don't expect you to be Michelangelo or Picasso, or anybody like that. Whatever you draw will be fine. I just want to get a feel for how you work."

She sat motionless for a few moments. "I'm really stuck; nothing is coming to me," she said.

"That's okay, Emma, it happens a lot with folks who haven't drawn in awhile," I said. "How about this: If you thought about the path of your life, what would the weather be?"

"That's easy," she said. "It would be raining."

"Well, that image came quickly, didn't it?" I said. "What color would your rain be?"

"Gray, I guess," Emma said.

"Okay, how about just filling the page with different shades of gray?" I said.

Emma looked at the box of chalks. "There isn't any gray here," she said.

I suggested she overlap black and white to make gray. "Try to cover the whole page," I said. "Don't let any of the brown paper show through."

She looked as if she had more questions but began to work. I moved to an easel with a painting I had in progress, and began to work as Emma covered her page with white and black. When she finished, she said, "Maybe there should be some blue in this, too."

After she added a couple of different shades of blue to the gray, I showed her how to blend the colors with a cloth. The result was a swirling blanket of modulating gray-blues that covered the entire paper.

I stepped away from my easel and looked at her drawing. "Wow, Emma, this looks like a stormy place," I said.

"Yeah, I think the wind would be blowing pretty hard," she replied.

I looked at the swirling blue-gray and made a sound like wind. "Whooooooooooooosh!" I said.

Emma turned, smiled, and said, "Yep, that's it!"

I asked, "Can you close your eyes and just listen?" She nodded and closed her eyes. "Whooooooooooooosh," I repeated. Then I asked, "Is this a flat or hilly place?"

With her eyes still shut, Emma said, "It's mostly flat, but I think it's going downhill." She paused and then added, "Oh, I just thought of how I want the path to look. Is it okay if I draw more?"

"Sure, Emma, take as long as you need," I said

She drew a curving path that meandered from the top left of the page to the bottom right. She filled in the path with brown and black. She added trees and rocks on both sides, and then a fallen tree laying across the trail. To the right near the bottom, she drew a white candle with a yellow and orange flame being blown by the wind. Nearly half an hour passed when she pushed the drawing pad across the table. "That's all I can think of," she said (Figure 6).

I laid down my paintbrush and said, "Yowsa, it's quite a drawing, Emma."

"Thank you," she replied.

I said, "I wonder, if the rain could speak."

She looked at me with a confused expression and said: "I don't know what you mean. I don't understand what you want me to do."

I said: "Emma, try to imagine that the rain is alive. It can talk. Rain,

Figure 6. The Path.

tell me about yourself."

"I," she hesitated. "I am cold and wet, and I make it hard to see where you are going."

"You make it hard to see," I said. I waited but she did not respond. I thought for a moment and then said, "Rain, is it your job in this place to make it hard to walk on the path?"

Speaking for the rain, Emma responded: "Yes, I guess I'm supposed to make things difficult, keep things hidden. Because of me, no one wants to be here."

I said, "Rain, can you see the path?"

"Oh, yes, I see it," she said.

"Tell me about the path, rain," I said.

Emma replied, "It is rough, uneven, and hard to walk on."

I asked, "Rain, I'm curious about why you keep people away?"

Emma answered, "Better to keep people away than to let them wear out the path." As these words hung in the air, Emma looked away from her drawing and said: "This is a little strange. I feel foolish."

I could see tears forming in her eyes. I continued to look at the drawing. "Rain, you seem to be feeling something?" I said.

Emma shook her head, as if to clear it and pull herself out of the role of rain. She blurted: "I'm not sure–nothing. I don't know. I'm not feeling anything." Then she turned away from me.

I returned to my easel and continued to paint. "Hmm, you're right, it was really the rain that seemed to be feeling something," I said. "Let's try something else: If you could give the path a voice, what would it say?"

She looked at her drawing. "The path would say," she began.

I interrupted, "Emma, can you try to stay in first person, to speak from the path's perspective?"

"Okay , I am a path that leads down a hill," she said. "Hardly anyone walks on me. I make it too hard on them, and besides, I don't really lead anywhere, anyway."

I moved to a chair beside Emma, sat down, and said, "You said you lead down a hill."

"Yes, I'm all down hill," she said.

"Path, I see," I said. "Is this a tree laying across you?"

"Yes, I guess it was blown here during a storm," she said.

I asked, "Do you like it being here?"

"No, it keeps people away," she replied.

"So, you would like for people to come travel on you?" I asked.

"Yes, it's been a long time," she said.

"Emma," I said, "if the path could talk to the tree, what would it want to say?"

Quickly she said, "I'd tell it to get off me."

"Path, the tree is listening," I said. "You can tell it."

Again tears filled Emma's eyes. She took a deep breath and said, "Get off me; you are in the way."

Speaking for the tree, I replied, "But I am only here to protect you, to keep people away, to keep them from walking on you."

More forcefully, Emma said: "I don't want you here. You are just getting in the way. Now leave me alone." Tears slid down her cheeks.

After a few moments of silence, I said, "Emma, I don't know where your path will lead, but I promise I am willing to walk along with you."

As she dried her eyes with a tissue, she said: "I didn't expect to do this. You must think I'm silly to cry like this."

"Tears can be good, Emma," I said. "It's good to feel things deeply, even if the feelings are uncomfortable." Before Emma left the studio that day, she made an appointment for the next week, and she took her drawing with her. It seemed clear that she had decided to continue the art therapy journey.

* * * * *

The metaphoric aspects of this vignette can be considered from the perspective of an audience that has just watched a play unfold upon a stage. When one thinks of Emma's and my behaviors as scenes from a drama, one is free to observe and reflect upon the meaning of the performance.

Emma came to my private practice studio with the complaint that she often felt empty. I began by saying, "Welcome to the studio, Emma." My intent was to receive and greet her as she embarked on her journey. The word *welcome* may evoke a sense of gratitude, appreciation, and openness that sets an immediate tone for the work we do; images on doormats, above entryways to new spaces, and hanging on the doors of homes will likely be conjured by this greeting. Thus, immediately I encouraged such images by saying, "Welcome."

Emma initially made only fleeting eye contact with me. She began by telling me she had been in therapy with a counselor for several months when she was an adolescent. She said, "He was nice and everything, and I think it helped to talk to him, but it's been awhile, and now I just can't shake this feeling that there is something missing." This sentence seemed to convey the meta-message that Emma wanted more than just therapeutic conversation, that somehow she knew she needed more than words.

When I replay this scene of the drama, I see that Emma has already offered metaphoric communications. At this early stage, I cannot know the meanings of these communications, but I do pay attention to the impressions they offer. She hesitantly looked at me, but quickly turned away. This action metaphor has many possibilities. Perhaps she was uncomfortable with men or authority figures. Maybe she found it difficult to focus on any one thing in her life. Perhaps she was anxious to take in as much of the visual stimuli of the studio as possible. Her quickly making eye contact and then looking away might have been symptoms of shyness, or she might have done so out of caution regarding the formation of a new relationship. Of course other explanations were also possible.

As Emma's session continued, she told me about her past therapeutic encounter with a counselor. This verbal communication also may have had several meanings. At one level, she may have been telling me that she valued the counselor's "niceness." This might be because he was gentle or understanding with her. She clearly communicated the belief that seeing the counselor was helpful. Perhaps this was a way to express hope that I, too, would help her. Yet for some reason, she had chosen to seek art therapy with me rather than return to her former counselor. Perhaps this was an acknowledgement that she was aware that at some level, she needed more than the counselor could offer. Or it might be that for some reason, he was no longer available. Perhaps she did not want to return to him and appear to be a failure. There were many potential meanings expressed in just this first brief interaction.

Emma then added a metaphoric figure of speech: "I just can't shake this feeling that there is something missing." I listened to her words, "shake this feeling," again in my mind. Did this action metaphor imply her sense that she must shake herself, or that the uncomfortable feeling was clinging to her? As I reflected, I pictured Emma literally shaking the feeling that something is missing. I watched the scene in my imagination and tried to get a feel for it. Was the shaking a violent motion, an angry shaking? Was it controlled like one would shake a set of musical maracas in a steady rhythm? Was it a shaking like one would shake if she were wet and cold? I tried to listen to the sound of "shake this feeling." Did I hear the shaking as an angry growl or rhythmic pattern, or did I hear teeth chattering as the aural accompaniment? All these questions were possibilities.

The last portion of her verbal communiqué also offered a metaphoric image: "There is something missing." As I replayed the drama in my mind, I wondered if the experience of "something missing" inspired her to look desperately, like someone who misplaced car keys and is late for an appointment, or was this "something missing" a vague sense of being lost or omnipresent encounter with longing? There were many possibilities.

Emma then told me she worked in a department store and was attending college part-time, studying to become an elementary school teacher.

Again, many metaphoric images were evoked in this interaction. I tried to envision her working in a department store. She did not tell me what she did there, what department she worked in, or if she was a sales clerk, housekeeper, or office worker. Because she immediately added that she was attending college, I suspected that her work in the department store was a job, not a career. There was no excitement in her voice or enthusiasm in her facial expression as she spoke of the department store, so I was left with images of a job she did not find fulfilling. The inclusion of her references to attending college and desiring to be an elementary school teacher seemed to indicate hopes for the future and plans for her life that went beyond working in the department store.

As I thought about this drama, I refrained from settling on any one interpretation of the metaphoric themes Emma raised. Rather, I tried to open myself to the multiplicity of potential themes, and pay attention to all their possibilities. Having taken in all these potential themes, I asked, "What would you like to get out of art therapy?" Up to this point in the interaction, I had introduced the notion that Emma was welcome in the studio and would be appreciated here. I paid attention to the many potential themes of her action metaphors (the way she averted her eyes, made facial expressions, and moved in the space), aural metaphors (the tone of her voice), and verbal metaphoric communications. By asking what she would like to get out of therapy, I conveyed the message that she would be in charge of the therapeutic process, and that I was interested in her desires.

Emma replied that she was not really sure. She said a friend had suggested art therapy, so why not try it? There were many ways I could interpret that statement. Was she being vague and elusive? Was she questioning if art therapy was right for her? Was she expressing a sense of openness and reserving judgments? Was she really unsure, longing for something that was hard to define? The fact that she said a friend suggested art therapy might indicate some positive associations to the process. It would have been different if she said, "My parents think I should try this," or, "A professor at school said I should try art therapy." At this point in the conversation, I was taking note of many possible meanings.

With slightly different wording, I again asked, "Do you have any idea of what you want from our relationship?" I tried to convey an initial sense of welcome and appreciation of her desire for change, and so I wanted to see how she perceived my early attempts to interact with her.

She responded, "I want to really feel again, you know, feel like I am alive." Emma's capacity to say that she wanted to feel again seemed to indicate that she was feeling psychologically safe in my presence. Had she not felt safe and accepted by me, I think it would have been hard for her to say those words. Encouraged by her response, I symbolically began the art therapy journey by giving her a tour of the studio, orienting her to where the art supplies were kept. Literally, we began with a walk through the studio space.

I then said, "Okay, now that you have gotten a feel for the options here, what media would you like to use for your first task?" This question reinforced the notion that Emma would have choices to make in the studio, and in her therapy, the choices were hers. The meta-message was that she would be in charge, and that she would ultimately be responsible for the work we did together.

She selected a large sheet of brown paper and box of chalk among all the media possibilities, suggesting several explanations. It could have been that she had used these materials before, and was familiar and comfortable with them. It could have been that she was attracted to the size of the paper and range of colors in the chalk. Maybe the brown paper seemed like such a common, everyday material to her that she felt comfortable using it. It could have been that she preferred dry media over wet. Or it might have been purely random.

The first drawing exercise, to depict the path that had brought her to the present, provided a metaphorical opportunity for Emma to portray important themes in her life. There were countless paths Emma could have drawn, and yet she chose to focus on one particular scene.

Her initial response to the drawing task was: "I'm not sure how to start. I haven't really done artwork since high school." This response seemed to show a lack of confidence and sense of hesitancy, which is fairly common to people new to the art therapy studio.

I responded: "Don't worry about it, Emma. I don't expect you to be Michelangelo or Picasso, or anybody like that. Whatever you draw will be fine." In this response, I conveyed a quality of acceptance and welcome. I wanted her to know that her efforts would be appreciated and valued, and by extension, that she would be appreciated and valued. This response, however, was not sufficient to help her begin to draw.

She said, "Bruce, I'm really stuck; nothing is coming to me." This was a variation of "I can't draw," a statement often heard in art therapy sessions. It seemed to me that Emma's stuck-ness may have indicated an inhibited imagination. Rather than try to coax her into drawing, I chose to engage her imagination in another way.

"That's okay, Emma, it happens a lot with folks who haven't drawn in awhile," I said. "How about this: If you thought about the path of your life, how would the weather be?" By shifting focus to the weather, something all people experience, I engaged Emma's imagination in a way that naturally connects to emotions. For instance, people often portray a happy day as a sunny spring or summer; conversely, people tend to portray a sad day as rainy or stormy.

Emma's response to this query was immediate. "That's easy," she said. "It would be raining."

I replied, "Well, that image came really quickly, didn't it? What color would your rain be?" Through my response, I offered affirmation and encouragement of her capacity to conceptualize in imagery, and then followed with a question that helped her augment the image.

She told me the rain would be gray, so I encouraged her simply to cover her page with different shades of the color. She discovered there was no gray chalk, so I suggested that she overlap black and white to make gray. "Try to cover the whole page," I said. "Don't let any of the white paper show through." These simple instructions did two things: (1) Emma learned to apply chalk to the page; and (2) Emma could work without concerns for "making it look right" because there was almost no way to fail when the task was to cover the page with gray.

When she finished covering the page, Emma said, "Maybe there should be some blue in this, too." After she added several different shades of blue to the gray, I showed her how to blend the colors with a cloth. The result was a swirling blanket of modulating gray-blues covering the entire piece of drawing paper. By blending the chalk, Emma learned an artistic technique and experienced success. This simple artistic process was empowering and pleasurable. Her success was a small step toward gaining a sense of control and mastery over the materials, which in turn encouraged a feeling of control over her life.

I stepped away from my easel and looked at her drawing. "Wow, Emma, this looks like a stormy place," I said. I refrained from asking her questions about the image. I did not want to get into who, what, where, when, and how questions that could be construed as intrusive or interrogative. Rather, by commenting on the stormy appearance, I offered an opening into Emma's own story.

She replied, "Yeah, I think the wind would be blowing pretty hard." Rather than inquiring about events in her life that have blown her, I responded by looking at her sky and making the sound of wind, "Whooooooooooooosh!" This metaverbal response helped us enter the place she portrayed with a deeper experience than an intellectual discourse would allow; together, we could imagine the wind on our faces.

Emma turned, smiled, and said, "Yep, that's it!" Her three-word sentence validated our entry into her story, so I followed with, "Can you close your eyes and just listen?" She complied, and I repeated the sound of wind, "Whooooooooooooosh." I made the sound again and then asked, "Is this a flat or hilly place?" By doing this, the image of the path was no longer restricted to the drawing paper, but was in both Emma's and my imaginations. At that point, we were picturing ourselves in the metaphoric place that Emma had created, and by extension, we were also involving ourselves in a fragment of Emma's life story.

With her eyes still shut, Emma said: "It's mostly flat, but I think it's going downhill. Oh, I just thought of how I want the path to look. Is it okay if I draw more?" By saying this and drawing, Emma confirmed her growing investment in the image, and in a sense, her willingness to be involved in art therapy.

I said, "Sure, Emma, take as long as you need." This response conveyed that she was in control, and that she could get what she needed from art therapy.

She drew a twisting path that meandered from the top left of the page to the bottom right. She filled in the path with brown and black. She added rocks and boulders on either side of the path, and what appeared to be a tree limb lying across the trail. To the right near the bottom, she added a small candle with a yellow and orange flame that appeared to be blown by the wind. Nearly half an hour passed when she pushed the drawing pad across the table. "That's all I can think of," she said. Emma's expenditure of time and energy in creating these images validated my sense that she was becoming invested in art therapy. Perhaps the rocks and tree limb represented obstacles and obstructions. Perhaps they were symbolic of specific life events, or perhaps they were simply aesthetic elements that Emma thought should be in the drawing of her path. The candle might have been metaphoric of her sense of vulnerability, a symbol of her hope, warmth, or smallness in the world, or something else.

I laid down my paintbrush. "Yowsa, it's quite a drawing, Emma," I said. My intention was to express interest in her drawing and interest in her without interpreting the content of her artwork.

"Thank you," she said. This reply could have suggested: (1) She felt some sense of gratification at my response to her image; (2) she felt discomfort, and so relied on a learned polite response; (3) she recognized that this was a place where particular kinds of drawings would receive positive reinforcement; or (4) she felt disbelief because my response was not consistent with her own evaluation of her drawing.

I said, "I wonder if the rain could speak." Again, this comment is open-ended. In a sense, I asked a question without asking a question. It was important that I was not asking for an intellectual description of what the rain meant, but rather encouraging Emma to give voice to an element of her metaphoric image of the rain.

She looked at me with a confused expression and said: "I don't know what you mean. I don't understand what you want me to do." I was encouraged by this response from Emma because it let me know that she felt awkward, under less conscious control, and therefore might be open to surprising messages conveyed by her drawing.

I said: "Emma, try to imagine that the rain is alive. It can talk. Rain, tell me about yourself." In this response, I am accentuating the focus on the metaphor of the rain in her image. By wanting to hear it talk, rather than hear Emma explain what the rain means, we entered the story of the drawing itself.

"I," she hesitated. "I am cold and wet, and I make it hard to see where you are going." This cautious comment was, in some ways, Emma's first steps down the path to her own imagination. By giving the rain a voice, she was reaching beyond her rational, explaining mind, into the realm of her imagination.

"You make it hard to see," I said. I waited, but she did not respond. This often happens in the early stages of engaging persons in such imaginal dialogue: Clients get stuck and it is necessary to shift the conversation to another perspective. I thought for a moment and then said, "Rain, your job in this place is to make it hard to walk on the path."

Speaking for the rain, Emma responded: "Yes, I guess I'm supposed to make things difficult, keep things hidden. I make it so no one wants to be here."

I asked, "Rain, can you see the path?"

"Oh, yes, I see it," she said.

"Tell me about the path, rain," I said.

Emma replied, "It is rough, uneven, and hard to walk on."

I said, "Rain, it sounds like you protect this place by keeping people away."

Emma answered, "Better to keep people away than to let them wear out the path." As these words hung in the air, Emma looked away from her drawing and said: "This is a little strange. I feel foolish." In my experience, when people have been engaged in this form of dialogue and suddenly say, "I feel foolish" or some variation of that message, it indicates that they are beginning to feel strong, although perhaps unclear, emotion. Rather than get diverted by her comment, I continued to look at the drawing.

"Rain, you seem to be feeling something?" I said. Out of the corner of my eye, I could see tears in Emma's eyes.

She blurted: "I'm not sure—nothing. I don't know. I'm not feeling anything." Then she turned away from me.

I returned to my easel and continued to paint. "Hmm, you're right, it was really the rain that seemed to be feeling something," I said. In that response, I was trying to support Emma's effort to distance herself from the feelings that were arising, and yet also acknowledge that while in character as the rain, she did express feelings. Without discussing the comment further, I said: "Let's try something else. If you could give the path a voice, what would it say?"

She looked at her drawing. "The path would say," she began.

I interrupted, "Emma, can you try to stay in first person, to speak from the path's perspective?" Emma's effort to distance herself from the image by saying, "The path would say," seemed to be taking her far from her feelings, so I suggested she continue to speak in first person.

"Okay, I am a path that leads down a hill," she said. "Hardly anyone walks on me. I make it too hard on them, and besides I don't really lead anywhere, anyway." We were now back on track, engaged in the story of Emma's image. The next several interchanges are examples of staying with the metaphor of an image.

I moved to a chair beside Emma, sat down, and said, "You said you lead down a hill." By simply restating Emma's words, I: (1) reinforced that I was listening to her; (2) avoided making interpretive comments; and (3) kept the focus on her images and words.

"Yes, I'm all down hill," she said.

"Path, I see," I said. "Is this a tree laying across you?" Again, I am commenting only on the phenomena of the image.

"Yes, I guess it was blown here during a storm," she said.

I asked, "Do you like it being here?"

"No, it keeps people away," she replied.

"So, you would like for people to come travel on you?" I asked.

"Yes, it's been a long time," she said.

"Emma," I said, "if the path could talk to the tree, what would it want to say?"

Quickly she said, "I'd tell it to get off me."

"Path, the tree is listening," I said. "You can tell it." This was a moment filled with intense feeling. The enactment of this brief dialogue took us deeply into the story of Emma's image.

Again tears filled Emma's eyes. She took a deep breath and said, "Get off me; you are in the way."

Speaking for the tree, I replied, "But I am only here to protect you, to keep people away, to keep them from walking on you." This is an example of keeping the dialogue going, continuing to be in the metaphoric moment Although my comments were a responsive interpretation, they were based on things Emma had already said, and not on my own ideas about what her image meant.

More forcefully, Emma said: "I don't want you here. You are just getting in the way, now leave me alone." Tears slid down her cheeks.

After a few moments of silence, I said, "Emma, I don't know where your path will lead, but I promise I am willing to walk along with you." My goal was to reinforce that this was a psychologically safe environment where she could experience feelings, and that I would not abandon her.

When she dried her eyes with a tissue, she said: "I didn't expect to do this. You must think I'm silly to cry like this."

"Tears can be good, Emma," I said. "It's good to feel things deeply, even if the feelings are uncomfortable." It would have been easy for me to remind Emma that she had indicated she wanted to feel again, but I sensed that she would have been hurt by such a comment.

Instead, I supported the notion that feeling is healthy even when it is not easy. Before Emma left the studio that day, she made an appointment for the next week, and she took her drawing with her. It seemed evident that she had decided to continue art therapy.

* * * * *

As the first steps of Emma's therapeutic journey unfolded, she portrayed the story of her path. As she drew her tale, she needed me to see, listen to, and try to understand her images.

While I worked with her in the studio, I paid attention to issues of safety, predictability, and art making in the service of relationship-building. I not only looked at and listened to her story, but through my own artwork, I shared parts of my story with her, as well. If Emma and I were to gain anything from this shared pilgrimage, we needed to get to know each other. In later sessions, the mutual exchange of our images fostered reciprocal self-disclosure. Our imaginal discoveries led to the sharing of vulnerabilities, hers and mine. In the therapeutic art pilgrimage I, too, was a traveler; we were in this together. This helped me to be faithful to the painting of my tale, stay honest with Emma, and remain honest with myself. As we created our artworks, we came to know each other. We drew pictures and made paintings about our lives.

Chapter IV

THE STUDIO AS MILIEU METAPHOR

Inspired by David Crosby's (1967) song "Mind Gardens", I wrote this story.

A gardener had worked hard since early spring preparing the soil, planting seeds, watering, fertilizing, and weeding—all the things required of successful tending. Now, in late summer, the garden was flourishing.

The gardener was dismayed one morning when he noticed that several of the plants had been eaten during the night. He assumed that a rabbit had invaded his precious patch, so he built a low fence to protect the vegetables and flowers. The gardener slept well that night, sure that he had done what was needed to care for the plot.

Several days later, the gardener was again perturbed when he discovered a number of plants pulled from the ground. Clearly, the low fence had failed to defend the fruits of his labor, so he began to construct a high fieldstone wall. He worked all through fall and into winter until, at last, the wall solidly encircled the garden plot.

When spring came, the gardener again spent his days preparing the soil, planting seeds, watering, fertilizing, and weeding. He was content that this year, the garden was truly safe, and he was sure there would be a bumper crop to harvest in the fall.

You can imagine the gardener's consternation when he discovered that, despite the sturdiness and height of the wall, several of his plants were ruined when he arrived at the garden one morning in early fall. It was apparent that some animal had jumped or climbed over the wall. After giving the problem some thought, the gardener began to build a roof over the garden. He was so busy constructing the roof that all his vegetables were left to rot on the ground. "Oh well," he thought," at least next year, no animal will be able to harm my garden." By late winter, the roof was finished and the garden was protected completely.

In early spring, the gardener once again cultivated the soil, planted seeds, and fertilized the garden plot. After several weeks, the gardener was concerned that no sprouts had appeared above the ground. Nothing was growing at all. It was true that no animal could get into the garden to ruin it, but it was also true that no sun could shine through the roof and walls, and no rain could reach the ground. The garden was safe, but fallow.

It is important for art therapists to consider their work environment as a metaphor and conveyor of information to clients. In many unspoken ways, the therapeutic space communicates information to clients regarding the nature of the work of art therapy. There are three important aspects to consider in establishing a therapeutic milieu metaphor. The art therapy studio, office, or group room should provide: (1) an atmosphere of safety; (2) elements of predictability in the client's life; and (3) a milieu committed to art making in the service of creating meaningful relationships. Art therapists can do many things to shape the milieu metaphor to convey these three messages. Intentionally creating the milieu is one of the art therapist's primary tasks. Gussow (1971) suggests that what changes any physical location into a meaningful place is the process of experiencing deeply. "A place is a piece of the whole environment that has been claimed by feelings" (p. 27).

Foremost, art therapists must provide a therapeutic milieu that is

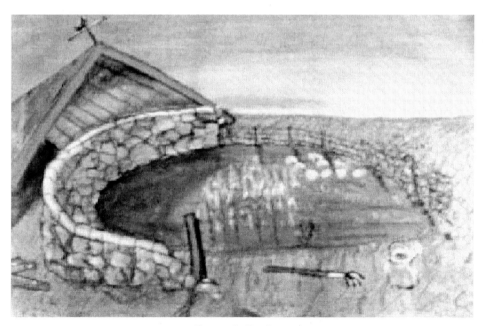

Figure 7. Garden.

safe and welcoming of clients' struggles. The experience of being welcomed and feeling psychologically safe is often a unique and healing experience for art therapy clients. In today's culture, people are inundated with overt and covert messages that pain and discomfort are of little value, and should be avoided whenever possible. The notion that life should be pain-free comes in many ways, including advertising, television programming, and other media. Although pain is not hidden the way it was before postmodernism, the exposure it has received in the media through pharmaceutical advertising, talk shows, and reality TV shows, has changed, but not necessarily improved the situation. A disturbing theme beneath these messages is that no one should have to endure discomfort, pain, or struggle; life should be easy, convenient, and fun. It is often a relief to the person experiencing emotional pain to come into contact with a therapist and therapeutic environment that acknowledges, honors, and accepts that life is difficult.

Two important dynamic elements in art therapy are safety and anxiety. People seeking help must have a sense that the therapy environment is a safe place to explore and share their inner lives. At the same time, clients need some inner anxiety to drive life changes. The metaphor of a teeter-totter expresses this dynamic: On one end is safety, and on the other end is anxiety. In this metaphor, the mid-point, or fulcrum, is the art therapist (Moon, B. L., 1998, p. 134).

Generally, clients bring with them all the anxiety therapy demands. Therefore, art therapists need to establish safety in the studio. For many people I've worked with, the process of creating artworks in the therapy context to express inner feelings is frightening. The pain and turmoil that lead persons to the art therapy studio can feel life-threatening. Against this backdrop, it is easy to see why psychological safety is one of the first required components for successful therapy. If clients do not feel safe, no therapeutic work can take place.

The presence of artworks on the walls of a therapeutic space has a permeating influence on ambience . The colors, textures, themes, and energies of artworks can impact the atmosphere. Images transmit creative energy that, in unspoken ways, conveys the message that the art therapy milieu is safe. The art therapy experience can be seen as a process of transforming destructive, self-defeating energy into creative, nourishing, and healing energy. One purpose of art therapy is to stimulate this nourishing force in the client's life. In a sense, the walls of the office or studio may become a dynamic gallery, always changing, restructuring, and reforming, thus providing a potent unspoken metaphor of the workings of the place. When clients enter the art therapy milieu, they are greeted by a host of images that invites participation in the healing activity of making art.

The attitude the art therapist holds toward the client and art making is also important. I find that clients thrive on the commitment and enthusiasm of the art therapist, which is easily displayed in our own artistic works. When art therapists actively engage in their own expressive art tasks, a positive sense of creative contagion is generated in the environment; it is powerful medicine. Creating this feeling of artistic contagion is up to the therapist. One cannot expect clients to generate artistic exuberance on their own accord; on the contrary, because the people who come to art therapy are often angry, hurt, and struggling individuals, generating artistic contagion is the therapist's responsibility. Artistic contagion is stimulated by the art therapist's ongoing commitment to making art, which is not necessarily talked about, but rather is lived out in the environment.

Other ways that art therapists show commitment and enthusiasm are through the use of their tones of voice, facial expressions, body movements, energy, personality, and charisma. Each of these personal characteristics can be important in establishing safety in the therapy milieu. Art therapists must exude some amount of excitement, expectation, and pleasure in their work, while also honoring the pain, boredom, sadness, and angst that clients often feel.

The art therapy milieu can also provide elements of predictability for clients. For struggling people to meaningfully engage in the difficult process of being in therapy, they must perceive the art therapist and art environment as safe, with the predictability of the place and therapist prominent agents of safety.

In some ways, this principle is paradoxical because art therapists are frequently surprised by the puzzling and unanticipated twists and turns of clients' artworks in the therapy context. While patterns and themes that emerge in clients' artworks often repeat, end products of the creative processes are impossible to know in advance. Art therapists can never precisely predict what will happen in an individual client's artwork, and yet are deeply committed to shaping and maintaining a consistent, predictable, containing environment capable of holding the unexpected results of artistic expression.

Consider again the metaphor of the teeter-totter: On one end is the unpredictable nature of the artistic process, and on the other end are the safe and predictable structures and routines of the studio. The dynamic interaction of predictability and unpredictability creates this paradox: While I never know exactly what will happen in the studio, I am assured that as the art therapist and keeper of the studio (the fulcrum of the teeter-totter), I behave in response to the creative expressions of clients.

There are many ways an art therapist can foster the predictability of the therapy environment, such as being on time; welcoming the client into the space in the same ritualized way; having the necessary material supplies and tools available and well-organized; being consistent in affect and attitude; using ongoing art as an element in the milieu; responding to clients' behaviors in consistent ways; and developing rituals of beginning and ending sessions.

These tactics and more give clients a sense that the art therapist and art therapy environment are safe and predictable. Clients can find comfort in knowing in advance what will be expected of them, and how the art therapist will be in relation to them. These elements of predictability establish the boundaries of the milieu container that hold the unforeseen, baffling, and awe-inspiring contents of the creative therapy process.

Perhaps the most profound gift art therapists give clients is art making. There are many helping professions that endeavor to treat suffering people. Among these disciplines are counseling, psychiatry, psychology, social work, occupational therapy, music therapy, pastoral counseling, and substance-abuse counseling. While each of these professions offers contributions to the lives of clients, art therapy has the unique advantage of being able to engage people visually, tactilely, kinetically, and aurally. In addition, art making involves the client and therapist in tasks that employ ideas, express feelings, and involve physical and perceptual sensations. None of the verbally oriented therapies have such easy access to all these possibilities.

As one considers the configuration of an art therapy space, special attention must be given to ensure that the milieu is both conducive to making art and focused on experiences that foster the development of relationships. Making art in the therapeutic studio is not merely a means to create objects; it is the ground from which relationships grow. In other words, art therapists do not form relationships with clients through verbal articulation skills; rather, they build relationships by engaging in art activities with clients. On one hand, art making creates an arena in which relationships grow; on the other hand, relationships create an arena from which expressive artworks emerge. Neither the art component nor the relationship component is more significant than the other.

By providing an atmosphere of safety and predictability, and making art in the service of relationship-building, art therapists establish a milieu that nurtures and supports therapeutic work. When safety, predictability, and art making are present, art therapists, working alongside clients, can genuinely look at, listen to, and respond to clients' stories. This looking, listening, and responding facilitates clients' artistic telling of their tales, at which point healing can occur.

Juwan Don' Do Therapy

For a period of time, I worked at a residential treatment facility for adolescents. I had to do a lot of thinking about milieu metaphors and my own art practice because clients here tended to resist linear therapeutic discussion, and the facility was not particularly pleasant. Some staff members treated adolescents as if they were prisoners requiring "tough love" rather than troubled kids in need of help. In this facility, the art studio and my own art making were the primary means to establish relationships. Let me take you there through a poem:

> Juwan don' like to talk much
> He tells me, I don' do therapy
> but this room is filled with color
> shards of lives cruel and hard, and
> there is darkness through the window
> washed in sullen gray green street light
> Juwan says there are too many holes in his head
> secrets from a past he cannot recall
> his fingers trace the mystery
> of undisclosed ahistory
> he is sure I will not stay
>
> And I wonder at his life
> the hunger and emptiness that brought him here
> all the hollow words from foster homes
> the words he did not hear

how the holes kept getting deeper
shadows and echoes
making their way
aching to be filled
the rumbling and grumbling of an appetite
never satisfied

He paints with such vagary
color oozing
sense of time losing
recounting rage he says, "how amusing"
and the holes in his head
just get deeper

He says "I don' do therapy, Dr. Bruce
     but it's ok to hang with you"

I look at this child and wonder
why'd they do what they did to you
why'd they do what they did to you

Juwan seldom looks at me
he looks the other way
streetlight through the window
he turns his eyes away

Juwan hates workin' big
I suggest that we work small
together we cut four-inch wood squares
we cut, we cut, we cut 40 four-inch wood squares
     wha we gon' do with all these, Dr. Bruce
     wha we gon' do

We're going to work small, Juwan
one block at a time
one color at a time
one feeling at a time

He begins . . . we begin
we always begin by
painting the edges black
one block at a time

one color at a time
one feeling at a time

Blue - black - red - metallic silver
all these feelings he keeps hidden
tumble and roll like a river
of pain and puss and passion
my words cannot tell you
of the violence and loss
of the unspoken cost

> There are holes in Juwan's head
> and I paint beside him
> one block at a time
> one color at a time
> one feeling at a time

Juwan, why'd they do what they did to you
Why'd they do what they did to you

He paints a candle of hope
and garbage cans on fire
what these mean I can only guess
haunting hints of a heart's desire

We paint love, guilt, anger, sadness, ambivalence, fear, happiness
loneliness, contentment, shame, hurt, reverence, horny-ness, lostness,
confusion, rage, desperation, hesitation, fascination, redemption and
defeat,
And I wonder
can Juwan's holes be filled by buckets of paint
am I a fool, or a would-be saint

oh Juwan, why'd they do
    what they did to you

Juwan does not look at me
he turns his eyes away
says maybe we get all these done
we could put'em together some way

Twenty sessions . . . 40 feelings
he tells me, I don' do therapy
darkness through the window
gray green light
too many holes in his head
a past he cannot recall
fingers paint the mystery
we do not speak
of Juwan's ahistory
he does therapy

four inches a day
he begins to wonder
will I not go away

Juwan was abandoned by his family at a young age, and suffered physical and sexual abuse in a number of the foster homes. Needless to say, he had good reasons to be guarded, defensive, distrusting, and resistive to therapy. Juwan's primary mode of resistance was to "lay low." While he did not cause any trouble with his peers or the staff, he also did not make much therapeutic progress. In some ways, the residential treatment facility was an environment that allowed him to maintain his emotional distance, and as long as he caused no trouble, he was allowed to drift along without making waves. He existed in a sort of emotional limbo, unattached, floating, and just putting in his time.

He was referred for individual art therapy because of his lack of attachment to members of the treatment team. In my work with Juwan, the art room became an asylum, a safe place: a sanctuary for him. I met with him once a week. Early in our relationship, I tried to interact verbally with him by asking about how things were going at school, what he'd done during the week, etc., to which he would generally respond, "I don' do therapy." But he did like art, and he seemed to be interested in the sculptures and masks that filled open shelves, and the paintings and drawings that adorned the walls of the studio.

Juwan exhibited an interest in painting, although he was clear that he did not want to "work big." During one session, I offered him what I considered to be a small sheet of canvas paper upon which to paint; it was 9″ x 12″. He worked on this for several minutes and asked, "Okay to fold this?" He then proceeded to fold the paper into quarters and painted intently the rest of session.

During the ensuing week, I thought often about the size limitations Juwan placed on his work. Because I typically like working on large surfaces, I found this irksome, but I had to admit that Juwan had appeared to be content when working with such a small surface. I decided to try to find a way to honor his desire to work small and my own desire that he focus on a more extensive expressive task. At our next session, I proposed that we cut out small pieces of wood upon to paint on. In the studio, there were several eight-foot-long pine boards that were four inches wide. Juwan suggested we cut them into squares. Eventually we made 60 squares, 40 for him and 20 for me. As we were working together cutting squares, Juwan said, "I think I'd like to be a carpenter someday." This was the first unsolicited and spontaneous piece of information he had shared with me. I left the session convinced that we were on the right track.

The next session began with Juwan gathering the squares and asking, "What are we gonna do with these?"

I replied: "Well, Juwan, I know you don't like working big, so I was thinking we might paint a feeling on each of these pieces. Then, when we are all done, we might put them all together somehow, or maybe just let them be apart."

"I don' think I know that many feelings, Dr. Bruce!" he said.

"Let's take it one block at a time, Juwan," I said.

He looked at me with a hint of a smile and said: "Tha's cool. How we gonna start?"

"I was thinking I'd say the first feeling and then you'd say the next one," I explained. "We can keep alternating like that. Okay?"

He thought for a moment then said: "Yeah. So, wha's first?"

Over a period of 20 weeks, we painted our feelings one block at a time. As Juwan put the finishing touches on his last square, he asked, "So, how we gonna put this all together like you said?" Each of us threw out ideas about what we could do with our colored squares. Finally, we agreed to arrange them on a large sheet of masonite we painted black. We placed the squares one half inch apart and the final piece was a mosaic-like panel comprised of vividly colored squares. Some squares were carefully chosen blended colors, while others held small symbolic images. The visual effect of the panel, with its black background and colored squares, was reminiscent of a stained glass window.

Through the activity of painting 40 "feelings squares," Juwan wrestled with expressing his ideas and feelings, and the physical process of applying paint. Note that none of the verbally oriented therapists at the facility had had much success trying to get Juwan to talk about his feelings or his life.

The relationship we formed in the art therapy space provided an asylum conducive to making art. As Juwan and I made art together, we discovered common ground from which our relationship grew. Art making created an arena in which the relationship could grow and graphically depicted feelings could emerge.

The safety and predictability of the art room nurtured and supported Juwan's therapeutic journey. I looked at, listened to, and responded to Juwan's metaphoric communications, and his healing began.

The therapeutic studio is the ground from which relationships grow in art therapy. The relationship garden in art therapy is cultivated as art therapists make art with their clients. The fruits of the garden are the images that grow as the therapeutic relationship develops.

By providing an atmosphere of safety and predictability that is open to the unpredictable nature of art, art therapists establish a garden that nurtures and supports the therapeutic journey. Art therapists/gardeners, working alongside clients, are able to genuinely look at, listen to, and respond to clients' stories. This looking, listening, and responding facilitates clients' artistic telling of their tales, at which point healing can occur.

Chapter V

METAPHOR AS POTION, PRESCRIPTION, AND POIESIS

Potion—a liquid dose, especially of medicinal, magic, or poisonous content.

> —From *Webster's New World Dictionary:*
> Third College Edition (1988)

I took me troubles down to Madame Ruth
You know that gypsy with the gold-capped tooth
She's got a pad down on 34th and Vine
Sellin' little bottles of Love Potion Number Nine

> —From *Love Potion Number Nine*
> by J. Leiber and M. Stoller
> (Lieber and Stoller Songbook, 1997)

I imagine that most psychotherapists are committed to the origins of their discipline as a "talking cure." A counselor once told me, "If it can't be talked about, it can't be fixed." This emphasis on talking connotes a superiority of verbal and conceptual discourse over other means of expression. According to Dewey (1934), "If all meanings could be adequately expressed by words, the arts of painting and music would not exist" (p. 74). McNiff (2004) also comments on the powerful role of verbalization in the helping professions and laments what he sees as the pre-eminence of language over other means of expression. "Because creative arts therapy has drawn its very grammar and syntax from the most conservative scientism, the introduction of the arts into psychotherapy has done little to challenge the dominance of abstract theoretical language in the field" (p. 123). Similarly, Hillman (1989) remarks on what he sees as the inadequacy of traditional psychological concepts. "Images and metaphors present themselves always as living psychic subjects with which I am obliged to be in relation. They keep me aware of the power of the words I work with, whereas concepts tend to delude me into nominalism" (p. 48).

Art therapists, and nearly every person who incorporates art making into psychotherapy, have experienced the capacities of visual imagery and artistic processes to open up communications, and tap into wisdom and insights that are outside the realm of rational dialogue. I view metaphors, in the forms of visual, aural, and behavioral manifestations, as medicinal potions that both express and contain psyche's therapeutic force. Artistic metaphors invite us to look at, listen to, and respond to them, and wonder about their meanings. Rather than assigning fixed interpretations to artworks, we reflect upon them, enter into their stories, listen to what they want to tell us, and make sounds, move our bodies, and create poems in response to them. These metaphoric responses are devoted to the continual process of drinking in art's medicinal, magical potion. Analytical observation and logical conversation contribute to art-based psychotherapy, but do not dominate the process.

Dora's Coyote

During the first several art therapy sessions, Dora, a nineteen-year-old young woman, seemed preoccupied. She had come to me because of her depression and her sense that she was too emotionally constricted. Although cooperative, she was so passive that it was as if she was just going through the motions. She seldom talked.

Her artworks, however, spoke volumes. One of Dora's early drawings was of a coyote curled up in front of the opening to a cave. The entrance was dark and ominous behind the coyote (Figure 8).

As I watched her working on this image, I wondered aloud what was happening in the picture. She said, "I'd like to go into the cave, too, but the coyote won't get out of my way!"

"It doesn't look like a very dangerous coyote," I responded.

"Well," Dora said, "he may not look it, but he can be mean, and he won't move."

Figure 8. Coyote.

"This is a really interesting picture, Dora," I said. "Would you be willing to use your imagination and interact with your drawing and me?"

She nodded. "Good," I said. "Now what I'd like for you to do, Dora, is pretend that you are coyote. I'll play the role of someone who wants to get into the cave, and we'll create an improvisation."

She closed her eyes and sighed. "Whatever," she said.

I began, "Hey, Coyote, what are you doing here?"

Dora looked up at me but kept silent.

"Coyote, didn't you hear me?" I asked raising my voice. "Why are you here?"

Dora pulled her legs up onto the chair, curling her body inward. She looked away. "I'd like to check out this cave, Coyote," she said. "Please get out of my way." Dora turned toward me and made a growling sound.

I leaned away from her and, with my voice trembling, said, "But I want to go in there and look around."

Again she growled and then snarled: "Get out of here. This is no place for you."

"But, Coyote, I want to explore," I said.

In a grumbling voice, Dora said: "Go away. This place is dark and wet, and you don't belong in there."

"But how will I know," I said, "if I can't get past you?"

The coyote growled: "You have no reason to be in there. If you dare to enter you might never come out again." Dora snarled once more, pulled herself into a tighter position, looked out at windblown trees, and began to cry. She said no more during that session.

* * * * *

Dora's visual, aural, and kinetic metaphors called me to look, listen, and respond, and wonder about meanings. Rather than assigning fixed interpretation to her drawings of the coyote and cave, she and I reflected upon them, entered into their stories, and listened to what the images wanted to tell us. In our brief improvisational interaction, we made sounds, moved our bodies, and created a drama in response to Dora's metaphoric images. In turn, our responses became metaphors themselves, committed to the practice of taking in art's medicinal potion.

The word *prescription* comes from the Latin *praescriptio.* It is most often used in the English language as a noun or adjective. As a noun, it means: (1) something prescribed, ordered, or directed; (2) a doctor's written order for the preparation and use of medicine, the grinding of eyeglasses, etc.; (3) a long-established, authoritative custom; (4) the acquirement or right to something through its continued use or possession from time immemorial or over a long period; or (5) a right or title so acquired. As an adjective, it means: (1) made according to; or (2) purchasable only with (Webster, 1988).

Fading daylight drifted through the dusty studio windows near the end of a session. I was sitting with Leann, a 17-year-old woman. She was signing her painting, an image of a large transparent blue tear with a jagged line of bright white lightning striking it (Figure 9). Deep red oozed from the wounded place in the tear, with all this on a deep midnight blue background. She'd been in the psychiatric hospital for several days and would be returning home at the end of the week. Home would be different because her father had moved out of the house while Leann was hospitalized. Her parents had announced their intention to divorce.

Figure 9. Leann's Tear.

Leann had worked on two paintings and a number of pencil drawings while she was in the hospital. It was time for her to go. I said: "Well, Leann, this is quite an image. You have done great work here in the studio."

She reached out with her left hand, brushing a piece of lint off the wet canvas. The tips of her finger grazed the deep red; they looked as if her painting had cut them. She made no effort to clean the paint from her hands. She said: "I will miss you, Bruce. Art reminds me that I am alive."

She stood up, took a long look around the studio, reached out her hand, and shook mine. I was left with a paint smudge on my hand, and the memory of her artworks and words echoed within me. "Art reminds me that I am alive," continued to ring in my head.

Haley (1973) believes that visual and verbal metaphors are analogies through which the therapist and client can communicate in a compelling and direct, yet safe and non-threatening, way. I wonder, sometimes, about the prescribed role of the arts as therapy in the world, and about the function of metaphor in such artistic prescriptions. Perhaps art should be prescribed.

I think of Leann's psychiatrist sitting in the office, scribbling on her chart, and prescribing art therapy. I wonder if he realized the power of what he was doing? Did he have any idea what medicine his directive would promote? Did he know that he was ordering Leann to remember that she was alive? Or did Leann's prescription have nothing at all to do with what the doctor ordered or what the doctor knew? Was the art prescription really about the legitimate claim to participate in the long-established authoritative custom called self-expression? Or was that prescription really about Leann's right to something through its continued use over a long period of time: her lifer? Or maybe the prescription was not a noun at all, but an adjective. Could it have been about "making according to" or "purchasable only with" remembering? Leann had said, "Art reminds me that I am alive."

It was true that the doctor had scratched his initials on the team treatment plan and prescribed art as therapy for Leann. But he could not have ordered, directed, grounded, or injected that prescription. It was Leann who became accustomed to self-expression, and Leann who made images according to the world within her. It was Leann who claimed the right to express her strong self and weak self, making art that cut down to the bone, struck with all the power of lightning, and dirtied her hands.

Poiesis: Creation or Making

Metaphors in art therapy are formed when the artist, media, proce-dures, and external environment intersect. Lowenfeld and Brittain (1970) describes this intersection in artistic activity as such:

> Painting, drawing, or constructing is a constant process of assimilation and projection: taking in through the senses a vast amount of information, mixing it up with the psychological self and putting into a new form the elements that seem to suit the aesthetic needs of the artist at the time. (p. 4)

The traumatic experiences that are often at the core of the emo-tional struggles that bring people to art therapy frequently have a sen-sual quality. Something happened: Vicious words were said; bodies were inappropriately intruded upon; deficits were endured; or rejec-tions were felt. The painful events that lead one to seek art therapy are visual, auditory, olfactory, and sensual. It would be a fallacy to imag-ine that such painful experiences could be worked through, resolved, or healed through talking alone. The success of therapeutic endeavors often hinges upon their capacity to involve the senses.

The research of Pfeiffer and Jones (1981) demonstrates that people learn more efficiently, retain information longer, and perceive mean-ing more completely when experiential modalities are engaged. Unfortunately, many therapies neglect the value of experiential learn-ing, relying instead on verbal interaction. Pfeiffer and Jones suggest that verbal interaction is one of the least effective ways to convey information, and that the meaning of the information may be lost in the process (p. 2). Art making is, in contrast, primarily a means of experiential self-exploration and self-expression.

Not long ago, people had to be involved in creative contact with the world on a daily basis to survive. They built their own homes, made clothes, grew food, and created their own entertainment. Today, how-ever, less creative involvement is needed. As a result, something fun-damentally human has been lost.

Therapeutic arts engage the senses. The artist sees the colors, hears the music, touches the material, and smells the oils. In this period of mass production, virtual reality, and cyber-relationships, the arts have the special mission of engaging creative sensibilities and working with metaphors that, as Lowenfeld and Brittain (1970) say, "make life satisfying and meaningful" (p. 13).

The depth of artistic metaphoric expression is integrally connected to subtleties of color and shade, emotional undercurrents that flow through line character, and physical processes inherent in the balancing of weight and mass. In art therapy, metaphors are often found in the physical procedures of making, and they are almost always connected to sensuality. Metaphors of poiesis revolve around sight, sound, movement, and touch.

As the director of a graduate art therapy program, from time to time, I visit places my students work. During site visits, I try to maintain a low profile, and focus my energy on observing graduate students as they work with client groups or individuals. Sometimes, depending on the nature of the facility, I am asked to participate in therapy sessions. This happened one summer semester when I visited a treatment center for adolescents.

It was really hot that day, over 90 degrees, and it was a long drive to the center. At that time, I had a Honda Accord with a broken air conditioner. To make matters worse, 97.1 Oldies Chicago was doing a musical tribute to the heat. I was bombarded with Bruce Springsteen (1977) singing, "'cause when we kiss, mmmm, fire," and the Doors (1967) singing, "come on baby, light my fire." Heat waves rose off the asphalt as I made my way across the parking lot.

Sweat was rolling down my back, and I wasn't in the best mood when Marianne, the art therapist supervising my student, said: "Bruce, we've been having a hard time with this group. I think the clients might do better, and I'm sure Becky [my student] would be much more comfortable, if you worked with us rather than just observe. Besides, I've read your book about adolescents, and I would like to watch you interact with these clients."

I was intrigued. "What's happening in the group that is giving you a hard time?" I asked.

Becky sighed and said, "Well, they hardly do any art, Bruce."

"What do they do?" I asked.

Marianne responded, "They come into the studio all wound up; we can hardly get them to sit down so that we can start the group."

Becky chimed in, "Then, if we're lucky, and can get through our check-in, they spend about five minutes messing around with the art materials. And then it's chaos."

Marianne added: "I've been working here several years, and I can't remember a more resistive group. I think it's because everything is so short-term these days. I mean, when I started here, we had kids in the program for five or six months. We really had time to develop relationships. Now, most of these kids are in and out in five or six days."

"So," I asked, "what do you want me to do in this group?"

There was a pause as Becky and Marianne looked at each other. Finally Marianne said: "We'd like to watch you work with these kids. You be the art therapist."

It became clear to me that they had talked about this before I arrived at the practicum site; this was a conspiracy. Although the air conditioning was working in the studio, I could feel myself sweat. We talked for several minutes about this, and somewhat reluctantly, I agreed to participate. "I don't want to lead the group by myself though," I said. "Just let me be a part of the team."

At three minutes until 1 p.m., as Marianne and Becky discussed their plan for the session, we could hear a ruckus coming from down the hall: The adolescents were coming! The group consisted of seven adolescents, three boys and four girls, plus Marianne, Becky, and me. By the time the adolescents reached the door to the art studio, the noise level was loud. Jumbles of raucous greetings were exchanged as Becky herded the clients around a large table with art materials in the center. None of the adolescents seemed interested in my presence. One boy, David, with a sort of charming, sarcastic enthusiasm only adolescents can muster, asked, "What are you gonna make us do today?"

A second boy, Sean, groaned, "Oh no, I hate this." One of the girls launched into a rant about one of the staff members from the unit. Another girl, Allison, said nothing. She sat, quietly aloof, seemingly oblivious to the commotion around her.

Becky addressed the group: "Ok, let's get started now. I want you all to meet my professor, Dr. Bruce. He is going to join us today."

Sean turned to me, "Are you somebody important?"

"I am an artist, and I," I began.

David interrupted and, turning toward Marianne, said, "So what are you going to make us do this time?"

Marianne said: "Today, we'd like you to just make something. You can use any of the materials you want."

One of the girls said, "I don't get it."

"You mean we can do whatever we want to do?" David asked suspiciously. "No theme or any of that therapeutic crap?"

"That's right," Becky said, "whatever you'd like to make."

"Cool," David said. "I need a new pipe." He reached for a handful of clay.

Marianne said, "David, you know that's against the rules."

This was just the reaction David hoped for. "No it isn't; Becky just said we could make whatever we want," he said. "There are no rules today."

Allison, who had yet to say a word, shifted in her seat and cleared her throat. She yawned and said, "Give it up, David; they always have rules." For a moment, everyone in the room was still. The atmosphere became quiet, tense.

Becky took this opportunity to say, "Ok, maybe for Dr. Bruce's sake, we could all go around the table and introduce ourselves, and say a word or two about how we feel today." (This was their opening ritual.) And so, one by one, each adolescent answered: "I'm Jeff, fine"; "I'm Susan, tired"; "I'm David, cool"; "Sean, bored"; "Cindy, pissed"; "Andrea, fine"; and "Allison, okay."

Then it was my turn. In my most outgoing and enthusiastic voice, I said: "I'm Bruce, and I am really glad to be here. I love to make art, and I love to be with people." An odd, awkward silent moment followed. I turned to Becky and asked, "Can we get started now?"

"Sure," she said.

I quickly selected a piece of 18″ x 24″, white tag board and some tempera paint, stood up, and moved to an easel beside the table. Arranged on the table were watercolor sets, stacks of various sizes of paper, craypas, chalk pastels, tubes of acrylic paint, jars of tempera paint, an assortment of brushes, and clumps of modeling clay. I began to work immediately with a thick brush and, within a minute or two, had covered the entire board with dark blue. By the time the adolescents had chosen their media, I had begun to work with black, light blue, and green to mottle the lower half of the painting. I was moving around, aggressively pushing paint, stepping back, and approaching: creating a dance with the board (Figure 10). I could feel the eyes of the adolescents on my back, and I could hear the noise level of the group diminishing.

It seemed that my style of engaging with the work, the energy I was putting into it, was not typical behavior in this group, especially not for the adults. My sweat was rolling again. All of this happened in just minutes. The studio session was only going to last an hour. In a sense, this was an apt metaphor for the adolescents' stay in the program; that is to say, it was short but all that we had to work with.

I pushed white and gray across the upper portion of the board. I stepped back, scowled at the image, and sighed. Allison, who was doodling with a pencil and watching me, asked, "What's the matter?"

I turned to her and said: "Oh Allison, I don't know. It just doesn't seem to be working yet."

"What is it supposed to be?" she asked.

I replied, "I am trying to make a picture of the ocean."

She said, "It looks stormy."

"Well that's good," I said. "That's what I am after. But it still doesn't look windy enough. What color do you think I should add to the sky?"

"I saw a tornado once, and the sky looked like—purplish green,"

Figure 10. Lighthouse.

Allison said.

"Oh yeah," I said. "That's it. Thanks." I immediately mixed in purple and green with my white and gray cloud colors. The other kids in the group were intently watching.

Allison crumpled the 8-1/2″ x 11″ paper she'd been drawing on. She asked Marianne, "Can I paint?"

"Sure," Marianne replied. "Do you want to work on the table, or would you like an easel?"

"Easel," Allison said.

Sean called out, "So why a stormy ocean, Dr. Bruce?"

I continued to paint. "It's like my life Sean," I said.

"Huh?" he said.

"Like I said in the beginning of the group, I love to make art, and I love to be with people like you," I said. "It's what I do, making art and being with people like you guys. Let me tell you, I've worked in places like this before, and I know how it is being in a program like this. I know you did not come here because of all the sunshine in your life."

He sneered: "How do you know that? You just met us."

"Oh, Sean, nobody comes here for a vacation," I said. "It isn't that nice a place. No, usually people come because of the storms in their lives."

Susan looked up from the table. She'd been swirling craypas around on a piece of off-white drawing paper. "Maybe that's what this is," she said. I turned to her. She went on, "These are like the clouds in my head." She laughed.

I took her seriously. I stepped over to the table, looked at her swirling colors. "Yowsa, it would be hard to have that going on inside my head," I said.

"It makes me tired," she replied.

Allison had covered her tag board with dark blue. She asked, "What should I do next?"

"I don't know, Allison," I said. "What are you trying to create here?"

She answered, "I want a stormy ocean, too."

David spoke, "Only storm in my life would be a dust storm like out in the desert."

Sean disparaged him. "Angel dust you mean," he said.

Cindy blurted, "Wasn't there a war or something called Desert Storm?"

Allison turned toward David and asked, "Why don't you try to paint it?"

"I don't have a clue how to paint," he said.

I said: "David, Becky is a good painter; let her help you get started. And yes, Cindy, there was a war operation called Desert Storm."

David said, "Painting a war would be all right."

Andrea reached for a piece of tag board and said, "I wanna do my storm, too."

To my painting, I added a beach with white rolling waves crashing onto the shore and a lighthouse. A yellow-white beam of light reached out across the dark roiling clouds of my stormy sky. Allison had moved her easel in order to be next to me. Fine Jeff, tired Susan, cool David, bored Sean, pissed Cindy, fine Andrea, and okay Allison—everyone was working on images of their own personal storms. Some drew, some painted, and one carved into a slab of clay.

Around 1:35, I became aware of how quiet it was in the studio. I listened. I heard breathing, brushes pushing against masonite boards, chalk scraping across papers, and feet shuffling. No one was talking.

At 1:48, Allison asked, "What do you think of my painting?" I moved toward her to get a better look. There was no land in sight, and yet a shaft of light stretched into her night sky. On the far side, an orange life raft was drifting with a small, dark figure upon it.

I tried to make the sound of a foghorn.

Allison asked, "What's that?"

"It's a foghorn to help the person in the raft make it to shore," I said. The room was intense and yet calm.

At 1:52, Marianne announced that it was time to clean up. A collective groan arose; I, too, lamented that it was time to stop. Brushes were cleaned and materials were returned to the center of the table. Sponges filled with soapy water slogged up paint splatters and clay smears. David, with no sarcasm in his voice, asked, "What are we gonna do tomorrow?"

Sean said, "I want to keep working on this."

Allison asked, "Will you be here again?"

Cindy said, "This was cool."

I agreed, "It was cool."

Poiesis—to make. So much happened during this 60-minute sliver of time; I wish I had a videotape. How do I explain that a group of seven troubled adolescents who had been giving Marianne and Becky such a hard time by just messing around with materials got so caught up in their collective work? How did the group shift from its position of, "What are you gonna make us do?" to "I want to keep working on this!"

One thing that happened was that the visual metaphor of storms resonated with the adolescents and made sense. As Lowenfeld and Brittain (1970) would say, painting and drawing immersed the adolescents in a process of assimilation and projection: taking in through the senses, mixing it up with their psychological selves, and putting it into a new form. Each resistive adolescent had indeed weathered turbulent emotional storms. The sensual process of making art immersed all seven in a profound experience of self-expression, and it felt good! The soul of the place (another metaphor) was ignited, and an atmosphere of artistic contagion was created. Allison's desolate drifting did not darken the lighthouse beacon. I was not declared the enemy in David's war. Susan's swirling clouds did not blow us away. I know this sounds corny, but I had faith that if we could metaphorically engage the adolescents and get them to really touch the materials, they would make art. It was as simple and complicated as that.

A Venture of Making

Phillip, a burly man in his early 30s who always seemed to frown, was referred to my art therapy studio because, as he put it, his life was a mess. During our first session, he told me that he did not want to be in art therapy "or any other kind of therapy for that matter." When I asked him why he was here, he said, "My family has me in a vice, and they won't let up unless I do this." The image of being in a vice was an intriguing verbal metaphor that helped me understand the pressure he was feeling.

My first impression was that he was a moody, ill-tempered man who was angry about being coerced into therapy. Phillip had been treated for alcoholism in a 12-step program for several weeks the previous year, and although he was maintaining sobriety, he still felt bad about himself. For nearly 20 minutes of our initial session, he sat rigidly in the chair, scowling at the floor. I made several attempts to engage him in art making and conversation, but he turned aside my efforts, and so I worked on my own painting. His manner and affect suggested that attempting to cajole him into participating would lead me nowhere. I

Figure 11. Building the House.

decided to avoid the power struggle; I did not want to become another vice-like figure in his world. For most of the session, he brooded in silence, as I painted two people building a house (Figure 11).

Near the end of the session, having watched me for some time, Phillip asked, "Why are you painting that?"

I stepped back from my easel, but kept the focus of my attention on the painting. "I guess I try to paint things that are important to me," I said.

He sneered, "What's so important about being an underpaid carpenter?"

"Oh, it's not about being paid, Phillip," I said. "These people are building the house for free." I explained to him that my wife and I had built a log home several years ago, and the people in this picture and I used to be close.

"Used to be?" he said.

"Yeah, but one of them died, and I seem to have drifted apart from the other," I said.

Phillip asked, "Why?"

"It's hard to explain," I said. "I guess things just happen that way in life sometimes."

"I don't get it," Phillip said. "If this is sad, if this stuff bothers you, why are you painting it?"

I replied: "Phillip, that's just it. For me, that is what art is all about: painting my life, the stuff that is hard and the things that are good."

He sat quietly for a few minutes. Then he gestured toward my painting and said, "I've been in a log cabin."

"One thing I like about this painting is that I can almost hear the sounds of the sledge hammer and feel the sun on my back," I said.

"I remember the smell of the one I was in," Phillip said.

"Yes, log homes have a great smell," I agreed.

He said, "That must have been a lot of hard work."

"Yes it was," I said. "Maybe I could paint in somebody doing lighter work."

Phillip laughed. "I don't mean you should change it," he said.

"I know you don't," I replied. "But I could change it if I wanted to. I always tell people that painting is a little like life: If you don't like the picture, you can just paint over it, change it, and make it the way you want."

"That's an interesting thought," he said.

I painted for a couple of minutes before I asked, "Are there any things in your life that you'd like to change?"

Phillip thought for a moment and said: "I worked at the same job for over 10 years, and I hated it. Three weeks ago, I got laid off, and now I have no idea what I'm going to do. My wife is on my case about it, and my kids avoid me. Basically, like I said, my life is a mess."

"Sounds pretty harsh, Phillip," I said.

"Yeah, yeah it is," he said. He watched me for a few moments and added, "You are a good painter."

"Thanks, Phillip," I said. "Painting is good for me. Would you like to learn?"

"I don't know," he said. "I haven't done any art since I was a kid, and I've never painted."

"Phillip, lots of people struggle when they first try to paint," I said. "Don't worry about it. I tell you what: We are almost out of time today, so between now and next week, I'd like you to think about whether or not you want to try. You might also begin to think about what you'd like to paint."

When Phillip arrived for the next session, he was carrying a small pad of drawing paper. He opened it and handed it to me. "I think I'd like to try to paint this," he said.

The image appeared to be a recently mown hayfield. Small trees were drawn at the horizon line. Clouds swirled in the sky above.

I said: "All right, I can almost smell the hay. Would it be a warm day or cold day?"

"Warm, I guess," he said.

The drawing stirred tension in me as I looked at it. It was empty yet also filled with possibilities. I said, "I wonder what will grow in this field next." I placed his hayfield drawing on the floor between our two chairs.

Phillip looked down at his drawing. "I'm not sure about that," he said. "For some reason, this picture just came to mind." He looked around at the other drawings and paintings that hung on the walls of the studio, artifacts of past and present clients. He asked, "How do I start on my painting?"

I replied, "Today we are going to build the frame and stretch your canvas, and if we have time, we can prime it with gesso."

With little enthusiasm, he said, "But I thought I'd be painting."

"Let's take things one step at a time, Phillip," I said. I pulled two 2 x 2s from the wood rack. "What size do you want this painting to be?"

"Mmmm, how about two feet long?" he said.

I handed him a tape measure and pencil. "Measure your pieces and make a mark," I said.

When he had finished marking the wood, he asked, "Now what?"

We moved to the miter saw, and I said, "Set the angle for 45 degrees and cut the ends of your 2 x 2s."

He approached the saw with hesitation. It was clear he hadn't used this type of handsaw before. He wasn't sure where to put the wood, how to set the angle device of the saw, or how to place his hands so that he could both maneuver the saw and hold the piece of wood tightly against the back wall of the miter box.

I stood beside him and showed him how to set the angle and position the wood. He began to pull the saw cautiously. "You have to pull a little harder than that Phillip," I said. "It won't bite you."

Without looking up, he replied, "I've never done this before."

"You are doing okay, Phillip," I said. "I know you can do it; I have faith in you."

When he'd made all the cuts, I suggested that he use coarse sandpaper to smooth the edges.

He looked irritated and said, "But these aren't going to show, are they?"

"That's right, nobody will ever see them," I said. "But the pieces will fit together better if you do this, and you will know that you did it right. There is no substitute for quality work."

"This is taking a long time," he said with a sigh. "I thought you told me I'd be painting today."

I continued to work on the stretcher frame I was building. "Phillip, building the canvas takes patience," I said. "Many art processes take time."

"But I've seen canvases for sale in stores," he said. "It would have been a lot faster just to buy one."

"But how would that be helpful to you, Phillip?" I asked.

"Maybe I'd have fewer blisters," he said with a laugh.

"Phillip, if you use a store bought canvas, you remove yourself from the process; you miss the opportunity to be in touch with the soul of the painting," I said.

He looked at me a little peculiarly but kept working. When he was done sanding, we fastened one of the pieces firmly in a vice and then, using a corner clamp, secured a second piece to the first and nailed the two pieces together. The processes of clamping and nailing were repeated until he had constructed the rectangular stretcher frame. After the last nail was in place, he inspected his handiwork. He seemed proud of his efforts.

"Now the canvas?" he asked.

"No," I said. "Before we stretch the canvas, let's check all the corners to make sure they are square and then make angle braces so the frame won't get knocked out of shape when we pull the canvas."

When we completed all this, Phillip's hour was nearly over. In many ways, this session set the tone for the rest of his therapeutic work. Our relationship often focused on the task at hand: sawing wood, using the vice, stretching canvas, learning painting techniques, framing the finished work, and affixing hanging wire on the back of it. At every step in the process, from gathering tools and materials, to signing and displaying his finished products, we paid attention to the metaphors

Figure 12. Hayfield.

inherent in the sight, smell, and feel of the work, as well as those contained in the images he created (Figure 12).

He came bearing his emptiness and the vice-like pressure of his "messy" life. Helping him develop a more positive view of himself by engaging him in the metaphors of creating was crucial. The tasks of poiesis, along with self-expression through art, were the treatment of choice for Phillip. The therapy was creating art together. In doing this, Phillip experienced the healing effects of expressive arts processes and developed a genuinely more positive internal view of himself, as I helped him work with and gain mastery over materials and practices. He sometimes made mistakes as he painted and got frustrated, but with encouragement, he always managed to back up and rework a section until he was satisfied. I think this also describes what Phillip was doing intra-psychically. He learned to view himself as "quality work." He learned to like what he saw, both on the canvas and in the mirror. He made errors and became irritated, but was able to slow down and remake his self-image.

This work could not have been done in therapy that relied solely on talking. It was vital that Phillip encounter himself through the metaphoric, active, and sensual experiences of making art. There was therapeutic value in the relationship we developed and talking we did, but it is essential that our conversations be understood in the context of the activities in which we engaged. Our relationship was bound to active and sensual creative processes. It was in the context of the studio that our relationship existed, and it would not have been the same without the sweat, blisters, sights, and smells. We worked simultaneously with Phillip's senses, his images, the process, the materials, and his view of himself.

Chapter VI

BEHAVIORAL METAPHORS:
SELF-PORTRAITURE BY DOING

If people's lives are defined as the sums of all their thoughts, feelings, beliefs, actions, and relationships, then arguably each of these elements may be viewed separately as partial self-portraits. In this chapter, I explore the notion of behaviors as metaphors of self. The inherent wisdom is reflected in the truism, "Actions speak louder than words." As one of my adolescent clients says, "Can you walk the walk?"

In art therapy, action is essential to treatment. Art is a natural action language for many people. My mentor, Don Jones, one of the pioneers of art therapy in America, repeatedly cautioned me to always respond, but never react, to clients' behaviors. If we think of clients' actions as performance art, then we are free to observe, respond to, and think about the meanings of the performance without judging or negatively labeling behaviors.

In many ways, relationships in art therapy are like ongoing performances. Commenting on this perspective, C. H. Moon (2002) writes, "The text and action stories of clients, their anecdotes and behaviors, provide the art therapist with an avenue of understanding that is sympathetic to an artistic perspective" (p. 103). The meanings of events are uncovered through behaviors. The client "tries out" for different parts within the drama. The client is the main character in the play and is also in charge of casting, set design, costuming, music selection, script revision, and choreography. Each of these functions is a metaphorical expression of the inexpressible.

Run, Jeremy, Run

Jeremy was 11 years old when his parents brought him to my private practice for an evaluation session. His mother was worried because Jeremy was having trouble in school. She said that although Jeremy had never done well in school because of learning difficulties, he had always been well-behaved. This year, however, his behaviors in the classroom were a problem. He was belligerent toward his teacher, got in several fights with peers, and refused to do most of his homework. Jeremy's father also shared with me that over the summer, Jeremy ran away from home. "I just don't get it," his father said. "Jeremy has everything a kid could want." This runaway episode, coupled with Jeremy's problems at school, prompted his parents to seek help. Jeremy's mother also said that there had been "a little stress in the house lately" because her husband, who received a significant promotion at work, was now on the road and away from home several nights a week.

During my first session with Jeremy, I administered a projective art-assessment. One of the drawings he created responded to my request that he portray both a good memory and bad memory from his life. Using markers, Jeremy divided his paper in half with a thick, colorful line. On the left, he drew a boy sitting in a large grassy field. A round orange sun was centered in the clear blue sky above him. Beneath this image, he wrote, "Summertime." On the right, he used dark colors to draw the doors to a building he labeled, "School." In front of the large doors, he added a small figure wearing a backpack. At the bottom, he printed, "First Day of School" (Figure 13).

When I asked Jeremy to tell me a story about his good- and bad-memory drawings, he stood up, turned away from me, and said: "This is a mystery story. You have to figure it out yourself." I tried a couple of other techniques to engage him in talking about his artwork, but he stuck with the message, "figure it out yourself."

Prior to our next appointment, Jeremy's mother called to say that things were still not going well at school or at home. "We have to do something!" she said. "Things can't go on this way."

When the time came for Jeremy's session, his mother was at the studio door, but Jeremy wasn't. She looked harried and said: "Hello, Bruce. I am sorry, but he won't come in."

"Where is he?" I asked.

Figure 13. First Day of School.

"Somewhere around the back of the building," she said. "He got out of the car and then just headed in the opposite direction. I wanted to pick him up and drag him over here."

Acting as if I were witnessing performance art, I said: "You did well by not forcing him to come to the studio. Why don't you have a seat in the waiting area, and I will go see what I can do." I went back into the studio and gathered two drawing boards, paper, and some colored pencils.

As I was heading toward the back of the building, Jeremy's mother asked, "What are you going to do?"

I replied, "I am not certain, but first I think I will just try to be where he is."

As Jeremy's mother headed to the waiting room, I looked for Jeremy. I found him sitting on the grass, his legs dangling into the well of a window. "Hi, Jeremy, good to see you again," I said.

He looked up at me and said: "What do you want? I don't like it here."

"Yeah, Jeremy, I sort of got that idea last time," I said. "I've been thinking about the mystery though."

He half-smiled and said: "Really. Maybe I should call you Dr. Sherlock."

I offered him a drawing board and pencils. "Well, as long as you are here, I'd like to gather more clues to the mystery," I said. "Let's do some drawing."

He laughed and looked at me as if I were crazy. "Out here in the window?" he asked.

"I like windows, Jeremy," I said. "And when I was little, I used to pretend that windows like this were secret places where I could hide out."

Jeremy lowered himself into the well. "I guess I could draw in here, but I'll need a smaller thing to draw on," he said.

"Okay," I said. "I'll go get something smaller for you to use."

Jeremy rose and asked, "Aren't you afraid I will go someplace else?"

I turned toward him and replied: "That would be another mystery, but Jeremy, we are wasting time. Can I have your word that you will be here when I get back with a smaller drawing board?"

He looked at me for a long moment then said, "Yeah, I'll be here."

I brought Jeremy a small drawing pad and colored pencils. I was relieved that he was still sitting in the window well. "Here you are," I said as I handed him the art materials.

"What do I have to draw?" he asked.

"You don't have to draw anything," I said. "But I hope you will draw something so I can get some clues."

He smiled shyly. "Hey, I have an idea," he said. "How about this: You draw what's in my head, and I will draw what's in your head. Okay?"

I'd never heard of or read about an art therapist working this way, but I decided to go with his suggestion. "Great idea, Jeremy," I said. "So, what should I draw?"

He thought for a moment. "You should draw a tidal wave at sunset," he said. "What's in your head, Dr. Sherlock?" He laughed at his own wit.

"I had a dream last night, Jeremy, and the pictures have stayed with me all day," I said. "In the dream, I was walking down a long hallway, and there were lots of doors on both sides."

"Acchhh!" he said. "That's gonna be hard to draw."

"Do you think drawing a tidal wave at sunset is going to be a piece of cake?" I asked. We both laughed, and then we both drew.

When the day came for Jeremy's next appointment, I was disappointed to see his mother approaching without Jeremy again. I hoped that the relatively pleasant exchange Jeremy and I had the prior week would make things easier. Jeremy's mother said: "I'm sorry about this, Bruce. I thought he'd be better today. There was no arguing about coming this time; in fact, he was waiting for me in the car when it was time to leave. But as soon as we got here, he got out of the car and headed for the woods."

I tried to reassure her by saying: "Don't worry about it. Jeremy and I have talked about our work together as being like a mystery. I think this is just another piece of the puzzle. I'll go find him." I gathered materials and headed for the woods.

I caught up to him as he was meandering along the path a few yards into the trees. We walked in silence for a few moments. Then Jeremy said, "This is stupid."

"What's stupid, Jeremy?" I asked.

"I guess you haven't figured it out yet, huh?" he said.

"No, Jeremy, I think I need more clues," I said.

We came to a bench, and I sat down and opened my sketchbook. "What am I supposed to draw today?" I asked.

Jeremy looked irritated, but he sat down beside me. "Maybe you should draw a forest fire," he said, making a show of looking at the trees around us. He added, "Like maybe draw this place on fire."

"Okay," I said. "I'll work on drawing fire. You draw an ocean and beach."

* * * * *

The next several sessions proceeded in much the same way. I would search for Jeremy, and eventually, we would find a place to settle in and draw what was in the other person's head. Especially interesting to me was that my searching time gradually decreased, and our drawing time increased. As our relationship grew, his mother reported fewer incidents of disruptive behavior at home and school. It was imperative during our searching-for-clues encounters that I make every effort to accept Jeremy's behavior and not react in a punitive or shaming manner. It seemed clear that he was, in some indirect way, trying to tell me something important about himself. Something was happening even though I did not know what that something was. For a long time, he continued to call me Dr. Sherlock.

After a couple months of sessions like this, I injected a new element into the encounter: I made sure that I was waiting in the parking lot at the appointed hour. As soon as Jeremy's mother parked her car, I went to Jeremy and said, "This time, you have to follow me."

"Why?" he moaned.

"Because today is backward day," I said. With that, I began to walk backward toward the door to the studio. Reluctantly, Jeremy followed. When we were both safely inside, I said, "You have to get the art materials out today."

He protested, "But I don't know where anything is."

"I guess you'll have to look around," I said. "Think of this like it's a mystery game." And so he did.

The self-portrait Jeremy enacted was about testing my reliability as an adult to see how I would respond to him. Jeremy wondered: (1) Would I follow him on his quest; (2) would I reject him; (3) would I try to punish him; (4) would I abandon him; and (5) would I be worthy of the nickname Dr. Sherlock.

After several months, he gave up his behavioral routine of walking away from the studio, and our sessions began and ended in the art room. Although we kept up the pattern of drawing what was in the other person's head, Jeremy eventually began to call me Bruce.

One day I asked him about calling me Dr. Sherlock. He grinned and replied: "Sherlock Holmes is the greatest detective of all time. You figure it out."

Viewing the sessions with Jeremy as if they were performance art, I began to suspect that his difficulties, what he had been running away from, were the feelings of loss and anger that had been brought on by the stress of his father's absence. These feelings were likely exacerbated by the beginning of a new school year and having a new teacher, coupled with the emotional turmoil that accompanies latency. One particularly interesting drawing Jeremy had me do was a portrayal of him standing in the school gym as several other boys were climbing a rope toward the ceiling. As he looked at my drawing, he commented that all the other guys in his class had somebody to teach them how to do things like that. He added, "I hate it; I feel so stupid."

Jeremy used both literal running away and metaphoric running away behaviors to tell the world how he felt. His behavior (action metaphors) helped him express his feelings and, at the same time, protected him from the pain and confusion he was experiencing from stress in his household and difficulties in school. The critical therapeutic tasks were first to be clear that he was trying to tell me something with his behavior, and second to regard Jeremy's behaviors as action-oriented self-portraits; this way, I could freely observe and reflect upon them, and respond to him in positive ways. Third, I had to plan a helpful, therapeutic response that honored the running away behavior as a significant part of the treatment process that helped Jeremy express feelings he could not verbalize.

Over time, it seemed that Jeremy's behaviors were about wanting to be sought after, found, and cared about enough that I seek him out. Moreover, he seemed to be expressing the desire for someone to figure him out—not just find him physically, but also find him at a deeper level, psychologically and emotionally. His calling me Dr. Sherlock suggested that he couldn't do it alone; he needed an expert to help him figure things out. At the same time, Jeremy seemed to want a partnership—not someone to tell him the solution to the mystery, but someone to work on it side by side with him as a fellow sleuth. When I realized that his process (walking away and then exchanging ideas for what to draw) was about me finding him and solving the mystery, I was able to genuinely attend to him whether we were in a window well, studio, or the woods.

The value of thinking about behavior as metaphorical is that clients' actions almost always speak louder than words, giving art therapists insight to clients.

Chelsea's Exit

I worked with Chelsea for a little more than one year when she was a client at a residential treatment facility. She was 15, in the midst of a deep depression, and diagnosed with Post-Traumatic Stress Disorder when I met her. Chelsea was the victim of sexual abuse by a male friend of her family. The man who abused her had known Chelsea for many years and been a trusted friend prior to the incidents of sexual misconduct. Chelsea was referred for individual art therapy because of her shyness and reticence to engage in relationships with members of the treatment staff.

Although she was uncommunicative verbally, she appeared to enjoy art activities. She engaged eagerly in drawing, painting, and working with clay. After a number of sessions with her, I noticed a recurring behavioral pattern: Chelsea would work intently with art materials and engage in casual social interaction during sessions, but when time was up, she would make a dash for the door without responding to my efforts to say goodbye, or cleaning up her tools and work area.

During this time, her artistic and verbal expressions seemed innocuous, and our relationship seemed superficial. It was difficult to assess Chelsea's therapeutic progress. For several months, the best I could write in my clinical notes was that she had attended the sessions and was involved appropriately in artistic tasks.

Gradually, Chelsea became more spontaneous in her interactions with me, and she seemed to enjoy making art. Still, the behavioral pattern of making a quick exit continued. I raised it as an issue during a peer-group supervision meeting. A colleague suggested that I confront Chelsea about her end-of-session behavior.

"I've thought about doing so," I responded, "but for some reason I hesitate."

My colleague countered: "Bruce, I think her behavior is inappropriate. By leaving the room so abruptly, she is being irresponsible and making you clean up after her. In a way, isn't that abusive to your relationship?"

"You have a point," I said. "If I got the feeling Chelsea was being hostile or something like that, I'd probably agree that she should be confronted. But, somehow, it doesn't seem that way to me. I'm not sure what to make of her behavior, but I think it has meaning."

After nearly six months of weekly sessions that proceeded (and ended) as described, Chelsea informed me that she wanted to "draw something important."

"What do you mean?" I asked.

"I've been thinking a lot about my mom," she said, "and, you know, him."

"You'd like to express some feelings about these important things?" I asked.

"Yes," she said. "I want to use some of those things [paint stiks] that you told me were invented to mark cows going to the slaughterhouse."

"I'm curious, Chelsea," I said. "Why do you want to use paint stiks now? You haven't shown much interest in them before."

"I don't know," she replied. "I just do."

Near the end of the session, as I always did, I said, "We have about five minutes left, Chelsea."

I was surprised when she began to put the paint stiks back in the box. She asked, "Do you need any help cleaning up?" Later, as she was leaving, she turned in the doorway, smiled, and said, "I will see you next week, same time, same station."

I cannot say with absolute assuredness what Chelsea's kinetic metaphors meant. So many questions can be asked. Some might interpret her reticence to engage with members of the staff as an expression of resistance and her shyness as a defensive coping mechanism. Did her innocuous engagement with art materials belie a tumultuous inner life? Were Chelsea's abrupt departures from the studio metaphoric expressions of her rejection of or fear of closeness with me, or were they tests of my patience? Were the first six months of our work together wasted? Or, perhaps, were all these behaviors expressions of a tentative invitation? Was she waiting to see if I would give up on her, get angry, or retaliate in some way? What did it mean when she chose to use the cattle markers (paint stiks)? Why did she wait so long to decide to "draw something important?" And why, on that day, did she stick around to clean up? Why did she turn in the doorway and smile? There are probably several equally valid answers to each of these questions. Although I don't know all the meanings of these behavioral metaphorical events, I am sure that Chelsea's behaviors mean something.

Behavioral metaphors allow clients to create fleeting self-portraits through actions that are louder than words. If we reflect upon enacted expressions as artistic events, we are free to observe them and think about their meanings. Art making is a natural action language for many people, and the relationships that are formed in art therapy are like ongoing performance-art events. In such events, therapists and clients can experiment with different roles within the drama.

Chapter VII

ART PSYCHOTHERAPY:
ATTENDING TO THE SOUL

E ngaging with metaphoric artworks in art psychotherapy involves art therapists and clients working with deep levels of thinking and communication. Such work offers clients the potential to grow and heal. In a real sense, images bring to light soulful portraits of the artists who make them. *Therapeuticus,* the Greek root word for therapy, translates to, "to attend to." The source meaning of *psyche* is soul; thus, psychotherapy can be described as attending to the soul, and art psychotherapy, then, is attending to the soul through imagery.

Attending to clients' individual metaphors in art therapy by responding with our own visual, behavioral, and aural metaphors instigates a process of image-evolution. In this evolutionary process, one image begets another and, as a result, clients' understandings may shift. This progression produces inner changes in how clients think and feel, and outer changes in how they behave in the world.

Eric's Roads

An example of the evolution of metaphors was observed in my work with a client, Eric, who drew an aimless road and stop sign (Figure 14) to express feeling "stuck" in regard to difficult choices ahead.

We explored multiple messages of the road, stop sign, boulder, smaller rocks, horizon, and sky. We wrote poetry, imagined listening to the sound of footsteps on the road, and as we engaged in the story of his image via a number of other metaphoric responses, other images emerged. One of Eric's later drawings, *On the Right Path* (Figure 15),

Figure 14. Dead End.

expressed a sense of clarity and direction related to his choices.

In this example, metaphor was fundamental to the art therapist's and the client's thinkings and behaviors in the therapeutic situation. The many forms of metaphor (e.g., verbal, visual, and kinetic) played important functions. First, the visual metaphors of the road drawing clarified the client's thoughts about his impending choices and feeling that he was stuck. As Eric and I engaged in dialogue with the stop sign, boulder, rocks, and road, particular aspects of his dilemma were highlighted. Eric's problem was reframed in a unique way that disrupted his previously held ideas and the behavioral patterns that kept him indecisive. His and my new ways of looking at situations via metaphoric expressions and responses also provided new ways of

Figure 15. On the Right Path.

wrestling with and solving problems.

Second, Erics drawing was unique, personal, and open to multiple interpretations. I engaged him in a variety of explorations of possible meanings for the metaphors presented in the artworks and refrained from making reductionistic interpretations. By doing this, I conveyed confidence in his ability to discover, in his own way, a number of meanings for his metaphors.

Third, metaphors in Eric's image facilitated communication about highly sensitive aspects of the his life without the need for me to be intrusive. The road, boulder, and rocks were emotionally charged, and led to Eric's acknowledgment that some of his assumptions and behaviors were contributing to his difficulties.

Finally, images of the road, boulder, and rocks became recurring metaphors in Eric's art that he found instructive in relation to several situations in his life. He was able to learn about himself because metaphors emphasize relationships between situations rather than presenting sets of isolated facts.

A Digression

A graduate of the art therapy program at Mount Mary College, Stephanie, told me the story of her encounter with the vice president of a major American hotel chain. The occasion was a healing ceremony she organized for her mother who had cancer. Stephanie invited some of her mother's friends to engage in a process of creating what she called "healing symbols," using clay and other materials. She hoped to provide a supportive environment for her mother. She was taken aback when her mother's friend, the hotel executive who was a self-described highly stressed and tense individual, pa used as he was working with the clay and said: "I feel calm. I don't think I've ever held clay before."

At the end of the session, the executive said that he had been caught unaware by the inner peace he experienced as he worked with the clay. He expressed gratitude that he had been allowed to participate in the healing ritual.

I believe the executive's experience of calm, brought on by his encounter with clay, occurred because the medium allowed him to slow down his life and take stock of things that were important to him.

A remarkable benefit of working with and through metaphor is that it encourages participation in soul. The poet David Whyte (1994) says, "By definition, soul evades the cage of definition. It is the indefinable essence of a person's spirit and being. It can never be touched and yet the merest hint of its absence causes immediate distress" (p. 13). Perhaps we often become aware of soul through its absence. Surely we have all encountered persons who seem soul-less, lacking depth and a spark for life. Participation in soul-life always leads into the depths of existence. It is in one's personal depths that the fire, energy, and inspirational groundedness of soul are found. Indirect metaphoric signposts mark the paths toward soul.

The meaning of one's life is one's own. Only the individual can discover and fulfill it. Yet in this, a paradox exists that although only the individual can create and fulfill meaning, meaning cannot be found in isolation. Meaning is always created in the complex interplay of the self and others.

The role of metaphor and art in the search for meaning is powerful. When people create artworks, they struggle with conscious and unconscious depths to free metaphoric image and give them life on the page. Artworks uncover both obvious realities and that which is hidden: that which comes from the distant past and that which is longed for in the future. The artist who allows the flow of imagery from self to proceed expresses with honesty: "This is who I am. This is what I am." Such self-expression often leads to a sense of peace, as was expressed by the hotel executive. Paradoxically, encountering the peace that comes from participating in metaphoric artistic activity can, at the same time, be unsettling.

Marcie Cannot Look Away

One of my favorite duties as director of a graduate art therapy program is interviewing prospective students. There is a sense of excitement and untapped potential in want-to-be art therapists I meet to discuss the program and application process. Prospective students often come to the interview filled with questions, fears, and doubts, and curious about the program and curriculum. They want to learn more about the profession of art therapy. They want to know if they have the requisite characteristics and personal qualities that will lead them to success in graduate school and beyond. At a deeper level, many of them want to be assured that art therapy is the right career for them. They know people who seem to hate their jobs, people who feel no joy or fulfillment in their occupations, and they do not want to find themselves in that situation down the road.

Marcie was in her mid 40s when she came for the admissions interview. Although I had spoken with her briefly on the telephone, I didn't know much about her. As we discussed the art therapy profession and graduate program, she seemed anxious. It is common for prospective students to be nervous in the interview, but Marcie's fidgeting and restlessness were more pronounced than typical. In response to her nonverbal actions, I began to feel anxious, too.

I tried to calm myself by slowing down and talking less; I wanted to allow more open space in our encounter. In response to a few moments of silence, Marcie said, "I suppose I should tell you about myself."

"Yes," I said. "What brings you here?"

Marcie took a deep breath and said, "I've always loved art, but when I went to college, my parents insisted that I do something that would be useful, so I got my degree in graphic arts."

I chuckled and said, "Parents have a way of wanting their kids to get jobs."

"That's right," she said. "Still, even after I got my degree–and I've been working now for 16 years–they never have understood my love for art. But, anyway, like I said, I've been working all this time doing things I should enjoy, but I don't. I go to work, put in my time, and crank out artwork for clients. It all feels so comatose."

I asked, "Do you ever get a chance to make art for yourself?"

Marcie stopped fidgeting. "Yes," she said. "Well, not too much, but you see, that's why I am here."

"I'm not sure what you mean," I said.

"A few months ago, I went with a friend to his church, and some people there were talking about wanting to paint a mural in one of the large meeting rooms," she explained. "On a whim, I volunteered to help. I didn't even know these people, but it sounded fun."

"Was it fun?" I asked.

"Dr. Moon, we're not done yet, but it has been amazing," she said. "There is a group of seven or eight of us working on it together. When I am there–I don't know–I just feel so alive."

"And that's what brought you here?" I asked.

"Yes," she said. "I want to make art that has some purpose other than to convince people to buy something they don't even really need." At that point, Marcie was animated but no longer fidgeting. Her whole demeanor changed.

"Marcie, it sounds to me like your work as a graphic artist has no soul," I said.

"That's it exactly!" she said. With that, her facial expression seemed to shift from enthusiastic to apprehensive.

"What are you thinking about?" I asked.

"I am a little worried about all this," she said. "I mean, I have a good job, great benefits, and good pay. I can just hear my dad saying what a fool I am to even think about giving that up so I can paint feel-good pictures with the downtrodden. And it's not just him; I can hear myself saying the same things."

"You have some tough decisions to make, Marcie," I said.

"I'm not sure—not really," she said. "I think I have already made up my mind. The pictures in the mural keep coming to mind when I am at work. It's like they won't let go of me. But, still, this is so scary. What if I make a big mistake?"

"How will you know if you don't give it a try?" I asked.

"That's what I think about when I am at the mural," she said. "It is almost like it talks to me, and I can't look away. How will I know if I don't try?"

Marcie eventually did enter the graduate art therapy program. She continued to create artworks that came from her depths, and she gave them life on the page and on the wall. Her artworks uncovered both obvious and obscure realities of her life. She allowed the flow of imagery to proceed from within herself and, in a most authentic manner, proclaimed, "This is who I am!" The images Marcy painted were often disquieting and disturbing, yet her self-expressions led to a sense of peace that, I suspect, no graphic arts salary or benefits package could afford her.

Chapter VIII

THE POETRY OF PATHOLOGY

Pa-thol-o-gy: The branch of medicine that deals with
the nature of disease, esp. with the structural and functional
changes caused by disease. From Greek *pathologia.*

–From *Webster's New World Dictionary,* 1988

"Normal psychology insists that this twisted insight is pathological. But let us bear in mind that normal psychology does not admit pathologizing unless dressed in its patient's uniform. It has a special house called abnormal" (Hillman, 1989, p. 150). In the introduction to Hillman's *A Blue Fire,* Moore writes:

> All of Hillman's work–theorizing, analyzing culture, practicing therapy–presupposes what he calls a "poetic basis of mind." This is psychology rooted not in science but in aesthetics and imagination. By taking everything as poetry, Hillman frees consciousness from its thin, hard crust of literalism to reveal the depth of experience. (p. 15)

In this chapter, I introduce ideas about the poetic and visual imagery of pathology, and offer an exploration of the metaphors of psychological illness as presented in the *Diagnostic and Statistical Manual (DSM) of Mental Disorders.*

For some art therapists, using the diagnostic categories of the *DSM* in treatment planning, documentation, and reimbursement procedures is necessary in their art therapy practice. The unpleasantness some art therapists associate with the *DSM* typically has to do with the process of categorization or labeling that seems antithetical to creative sensibilities and empathy. Nevertheless, assignment of diagnostic categories is a requirement in many clinical settings, and the *DSM* is the accepted guide to diagnosis, so it behooves art therapists to find ways to creatively incorporate the process into their professional lives. Outside requirements notwithstanding, the *DSM* has a history worth understanding.

The American Psychiatric Association publishes the *DSM,* the sourcebook most often used in diagnosing mental disorders in the United States. Some iconoclastic therapists have suggested that they use the *DSM* primarily for completing reimbursement forms for insurance companies that require a client to have a diagnosis.

The classification system and symptomatic criteria of the *DSM* are based primarily on the majority opinions of psychiatrists who represent American mental health specialists; however, the content of the *DSM* does not necessarily reflect all perspectives on the subject of psychopathology. A criticism of the system is that the diagnostic criteria are shaped by cultural influences, and these criteria require periodic alteration in order to reflect the contemporary social milieu; thus, what is and is not considered a mental disorder is subject to change. An example of the changeable nature of illness classification is that prior to 1973, homosexuality was considered a mental disorder.

In some ways, the manual is a historical and social record. Postmodern clinicians, deconstructionists, and other critics of the *DSM* argue that some people fall into several categories simultaneously, while other clients fail to fit into any particular category. Still others (often art therapists) complain about the effort they must devote to the arbitrary process of clinical categorization, and suggest that their time and attention would be better directed towards exploring the life events that precipitated clients' mental disturbances.

The most beneficial aspect of the *DSM* is that it provides a linguistic shorthand for clinical description and discussion among colleagues. Least helpful is when it is used to reduce complex and mysterious human beings to clusters of disembodied symptoms requiring cures.

Uncovering the Poetry of Pathology

One method I have developed that allows me to embrace the *DSM* is to poeticize the descriptions of various illnesses. By poeticizing, I mean to look for key words in clinical descriptions, reflect upon their metaphoric and imaginal qualities, and reframe these in poetic style. For example, consider the first sentence in description #300.4 Dysthymic Disorder: "The essential feature of Dysthymic Disorder is a chronically depressed mood that occurs for most of the day more days than not for at least 2 years" (American Psychiatric Association, *Diagnostic and Statistical Manual of Mental Disorders,* 2000, p. 376). When I say these words out loud, "depressed mood that occurs for most of the day more days than not," an image of an empty field forms in my mind (Figure 16).

As I consider this image of emptiness and again say the words aloud, "depressed mood that occurs for most of the day more days than not for at least 2 years," I am reminded of Sam, a client who was diagnosed with Dysthymic Disorder. As I think about Sam, a poem

Figure 16. Empty Field.

forms in my mind:

> For most of the day
> more days than not
> Sam does not raise his eyes
> he walks but does not smell the grass
> nor feel the wind on his face
>
> More days than not
> for most of the day
> Sam does not raise his eyes.

There is a wistful and lonely sadness evoked by the small phrase, "for most of the day more days than not." When I poeticize the clinical description, I freely associate with imagery (Figure 16). I then respond to the image with poetry. This process of poeticizing increases both my intellectual and emotional understanding of dysthymia and, at the same time, deepens my empathy for Sam and other clients with that disorder. With tongue in cheek, I suggest that perhaps the American Psychiatric Association should consider publishing an illustrated and poetically annotated version of the *DSM*.

To further illustrate the method of uncovering the poetry of pathology, consider #309 Adjustment Disorder. The *DSM-IV-TR* (2000) describes the diagnostic criteria for Adjustment Disorders in the following way:

A. The development of emotional or behavioral symptoms in response to an identifiable stressor(s) occurring within 3 months of the onset of the stressor(s).
B. These symptoms or behaviors are clinically significant as evidenced by either of the following:
   1. marked distress that is in excess of what would be expected from exposure to the stressor
   2. significant impairment in social or occupational (academic) functioning
C. The stress related disturbance does not meet the criteria for another specific Axis I disorder and is not merely an exacerbation of a preexisting Axis I or Axis II disorder.
D. The symptoms do not represent Bereavement
E. Once the stressor (or its consequences) has terminated the symptoms do not persist for more than an additional six months.

Specify if:
Acute: if the disturbance lasts less than 6 months
Chronic: if the disturbance lasts for 6 months or longer. (p. 680)

This description and especially the words "marked distress" remind me of a 14 -year-old African American girl I worked with several years ago. Angel was referred to me while she was an inpatient at a psychiatric hospital. She'd been admitted to the hospital several months after her adoptive parents had discussed her adoption with her for the first time. Her parents reported that prior to that conversation, there had been typical parent-teenager conflicts, but that since the discussion, Angel's behavior at school and home had become increasingly argumentative, and her grades had deteriorated. An intense argument with her mother, in which she had become combative, precipitated admission.

In the hospital environment, Angel was often belligerent and aggressive with members of the treatment team, and argumentative and physically aggressive with her peers. She was a client whom it was easy to dislike and avoid. Frequently, in meetings of the treatment team, there was discussion of whether Angel should remain in the hospital or be sent to a more secure treatment facility.

Angel's initial diagnosis was # 309.4 Adjustment Disorder with Mixed Disturbance of Emotions and Conduct. The DSM describes this subtype of Adjustment Disorder in the following way:

> This subtype should be used when the predominant manifestations are both emotional symptoms (e.g., depression, anxiety) and a disturbance of conduct. The manifestation is a disturbance in conduct in which there is a violation of the rights of others or of major age-appropriate societal norms and rules (e.g., truancy, vandalism, reckless driving, fighting, defaulting on legal responsibilities). (p. 680)

Like my colleagues on the treatment team, I wrestled with my feelings about Angel. I was uncomfortable harboring the desire for Angel to be sent away. Finally, I decided to write about my reactions to her case history and diagnosis as a way to work through my countertransference.

> Angel's world has shattered
> shards of shrapnel embedded in her heart
> no one can see them but there they are

everyone knows they mark her distress

stand close to her and you can hear the
splinters rattling in every word
Angel's broken world is buried in her heart

She says, My daddy was a fine man
my real momma was some kinda African princess

But the record says that
Angel's father is servin' time
and her mother was just thirteen
on the day she gave birth to this child
she didn' really know the father
she doesn't really care . . .
about the slivers Angel hides in her heart

She comes to the studio in the
fall of her fourteenth year
she has declared war
wants to drop out of school
wants to drop out of her life
she is always angry
she bangs her head against the wall
slaps her face with her small dark hands
till her face burns and her hands sting
yes, Angel's shards are buried in her heart

And it wasn't too long before
the thirteen-year-old African princess abandoned her
gave her away

Angel says, my mom and dad
say they picked me out
yes they picked me out
to do something good for the world
they make it sound like
when we go to Walmart
to pick out all the crap we don' need
You gotta wonder what they were thinkin'
they don't pick very good
I am nothin' like them

Mother says they picked me out
I think they made a big mistake
some kinda big mistake

Angel's world has shattered
shards of shrapnel embedded in her heart
no one can see them but there they are
everyone knows
stand close to her and you can hear the
splinters rattling in every word
Angel's broken world is buried in her heart

When I finished writing this poem, I had a new appreciation for Angel's plight, and a different understanding of her anger and pain. While I did not read the poem to my colleagues on the treatment team, I was able to subtly shift to a position of advocacy for Angel in our weekly discussions.

For me, the process of poeticizing the *DSM* is a way to enhance my empathic understanding of clients. While the experience of reading the diagnostic category provides me with an intellectual and emotionally distant understanding of clients' struggles, the creative act of writing poetry brings me into deeper emotional awareness.

What purpose does the process of poetic interpretation of diagnostic criteria serve? For art therapists who are working in contexts that rely upon the *DSM,* poeticizing can provide an artistic reframing of the linguistic shorthand that often reduces complex human beings to clusters of dysfunctional symptoms. Poeticizing the language of the *DSM* offers different understandings of people, situations, and relationships. It highlights pathos (compassion) rather than pathology (Hillman, 1989; Moon, B. L., 2005).

The process of poeticizing the analytical and rational language of the *DSM* may deepen art therapists' understanding of clients' difficulties, while at the same time enhancing their capacity to engage in meaningful clinical discussions with colleagues. Art therapists may be able to convey compassionate pictures of clients via poetic metaphors to members of treatment teams who might otherwise maintain more detached and clinical views.

Ultimately, the *DSM* is a tool art therapists may choose to embrace, struggle with, reject, or begrudgingly accept. Regardless of one's predisposition toward the tool, the *DSM* can be a rich source of poetry and imagery if effort is made to identify key words in clinical descriptions, and contemplate metaphoric and poetic possibilities.

Chapter IX

TREATMENT PLANNING AND
THE THERAPEUTIC ALLIANCE

THE PARADOX OF PLANNING IN ART THERAPY

Art therapy, like many activities, involves premeditation and preparation by art therapists. Early in the therapeutic process, clients and art therapists collaborate in the creation of distinct goals and outcomes for the therapy. Establishing clear therapeutic goals provides a context in which clients' progress can be measured.

Although I agree with the advisability of establishing understandable and agreed upon goals in therapy, I want to discuss three potential impediments to strategic-outcome planning in art therapy:

1. Art making is nearly always surprising and unpredictable. One never knows exactly what will happen when people paint, sculpt, or draw. Some artists begin their work with clear ideas about how the finished piece should look. Other artists have no conscious intention when they start a new artwork. They just get to work, make marks, and wait for Muses to inspire them. When making art, accidents happen: Paint splatters and drips, clay cracks, and chalk smears. Each of these unplanned phenomena has potential to change the visual impact of artworks.
2. Metaphors, by nature, hold in tension the potential of multiple interpretations. Art therapists, attempting to communicate with clients indirectly via visual or verbal metaphors, can never be sure if clients understand the points of metaphors the way they hope. Clients are free to arrive at unexpected and unpredictable interpretations of art therapists' metaphoric messages.

108

3. Many people referred to art therapists cannot or will not put into words the feelings and thoughts they most need to express. Therefore, art therapists must look at, listen to, and respond to clients in more ways than logical, linear discussion alone.

When the unpredictable processes of art making are combined with the multi-interpretational potential of metaphoric expression and applied to persons who do not readily verbalize, results can be complex and capricious. Thus, art therapists must operate within the paradox of attempting to form coherent treatment plans while accepting that much of what occurs in art therapy studios defies premeditation.

Our clients' (and our own) metaphors are created in visual images of snakes, monsters, barren deserts, paths, rain, fallen trees, tears, lightning, lighthouses, stormy seas, and wars. Metaphors are glimpsed in the ways pencils make marks, chalks are smoothed, and paints are smeared across surfaces, as well as in the ways hands push into and against clay. Metaphoric dances are witnessed as people enter a room, move to a chair, interact with easels and potter's wheels, tilt their heads, and avert their eyes. Metaphors are heard in the rustling melodies of chalk on paper.

Despite its metaverbal nature, art therapy is still a process of communication in which the ultimate ends, or therapeutic objectives, are important to define. Messages that emanate from art therapists to clients should be intended to draw out responses that assist clients in realizing goals. "Therapy is thus a meeting of therapist and client for the purpose of exchanging communications with a view to making changes" (Barker, 1996, p. 66). If every artwork a client creates is a metaphor of the client's life, and whatever a client needs to express is effectively communicated, one can understand how art therapists can design treatment plans, yet remain open to the vagaries of artistic and metaphoric processes.

Imaging Therapeutic Objectives

Persons referred for art therapy services typically long for their lives to be different. They come bearing stories of depression, anger, neglect, abuse, guilt, and confusion in hopes that their unspoken and, sometimes, unspeakable narratives take form and are finally understood. Generally, they have already tried talk therapy, but have not been willing or able to convey the critical themes of their lives in words; hence, art therapy is needed.

A constructive early step in the therapeutic art process is to create an image of the desired therapeutic outcome. It helps to engage clients in artistic tasks that metaphorically depict the hoped for results of art therapy. In early stage of therapy, clients may benefit from artistic tasks such as one of the following:

1. Draw a picture of where you've been, where you are, and where you want to be;
2. Create a symbolic portrait of yourself in relation to where you've been, where you are, and where you want to be;
3. Paint an image depicting on one side how you feel most of the time and on the other side how you wish you could feel;
4. Read Robert Frost's (1920) poem *The Road Not Taken,* and ask clients to respond by portraying the path of their lives. Then ask clients to consider where they want the path to lead; or
5. Draw a hallway with three doors: One leads to the past, one to the present, and one to the future. Ask clients, what is behind each door?

Of course, many other metaphoric themes may also be appropriate directives for particular clients. My goal is not to prescribe specific artistic exercises but, rather, to encourage an imaginal frame for creating and reviewing treatment goals. Images created in response to art therapy directives similar to those I listed invariably lead clients to share feelings and stories related to their hopes and aspirations. As art therapists interact with clients and their artworks, it helps to explore the multitude of possible messages that emerge regarding how clients' lives can improve.

Foreground and Background

In many forms of art, there are overt distinctions between the foreground and the background: the detail and the big picture. The same is true of therapeutic goals. Some goals are short-term and intended to be met immediately, while others are long-term big-picture goals. As art therapists work with clients to create images that depict the desired outcome of therapy, it helps to differentiate between short-term, intermediate, and long-term goals.

Metaphoric images can also motivate clients to decide if they want to engage in therapy. Dan, a client I once worked with portrayed himself standing beside a wooden crate large enough to hold a person. He came for several art therapy sessions but remained ambivalent as to whether he wanted to struggle with his problems. As he talked about his picture, he lamented that he felt "boxed in" by life.

I asked, "Would you like to get out of the box?"

Dan responded immediately, "Yes, I am so tired of feeling this way all the time!"

"Well, maybe you have to really get into the box before you can get out of it," I replied.

He frowned and said, "What are you trying to say?"

"I'm not trying to say anything," I said. "It's your drawing and, in the drawing, you are standing outside the crate even though you say you feel boxed in." Later I suggested that he not schedule another appointment until he was ready to "really get into the box." Several weeks later, when Dan called to make another appointment, he said, "I guess the only way out is in."

Metaphoric images can also help motivate members of therapy groups to explore aspects of their interpersonal relationships in safe, non-threatening ways. Sometimes, a carefully considered metaphoric task can gently cut through defenses that tend to disrupt a group's therapeutic work. An example of this function of a metaphor happened when I was leading a group at a residential treatment program for alcoholic women.

After meeting with the group of seven women for several sessions, I was frustrated by the superficial dynamics. Members of the group were adept at keeping the tone light: They gossiped and told outrageously funny stories, but subtly resisted all attempts on my part to "sober up" the tone of the group.

As I talked about the group with my supervisor, I told her I was frustrated and considering asking to be replaced as group leader. My supervisor responded, "It sounds like the group is lost in the woods."

At the beginning of the next art therapy group session, I taped a 12-foot-long piece of brown kraft paper to one wall. I then asked clients to select a piece of green, brown, white, or black chalk, and work together to cover the entire paper. "Don't let any of the brown paper show through," I said. As they worked to obliterate the brown paper, clients inadvertently (and unavoidably) bumped into one another. Chalk dust flew, and a pleasant hum of conversation and laughter arose that suggested enjoyment of the simple task.

When the paper was covered, I gave members of the group small cloths and asked them to blend the colors. The result was a mottled background of subtle shades of green and brown. Addressing the group, I said: "We have created a dense forest. What I want us to do now is draw ourselves into this forest. Portray yourself as some element or character that represents how you see yourself in this group. For example, you might be an animal or some kind of plant."

A flurry of activity ensued. One of the women drew an apple tree laden with fruit. Another portrayed a koala bear, and yet another represented her involvement in the group by drawing poison ivy vines extending across the paper. Like before, there was chatter and social banter. One of the women was markedly quiet as she drew a porcupine with bristling quills.

After we completed our drawings, we arranged our chairs in a semicircle facing the forest mural as we discussed the images. Predictably, an air of surface humor marked the conversation, and members of the group avoided serious consideration of how the images might symbolize roles that group members played. Comments were made about the "cuddly" koala bear, and how the apples would make great pies. When it came time for Brenda, the woman who had drawn the porcupine to talk about her image, one of the group members said, "Oh, that porcupine looks so cute."

Brenda chuckled and said: "Well, it may be cute, but you better watch out for those quills. They will hurt you if you touch them."

I said, "It looks like the quills are really bristling."

She replied, "Yes, they do that when they are threatened."

Another group member smiled and commented, "It looks like a character from a Walt Disney cartoon." This drew nods from other members of the group, and one woman added, "I just loved *The Lion King.*" That comment inspired several remarks on people's favorite Disney movies.

I sat silent for several moments, waiting for the chatting to wind down. Finally, the group sensed my stillness and turned toward me. Addressing the porcupine image, I asked, "Porcupine, your quills are bristling; are you threatened in this forest?" I turned toward the artist.

An uncomfortable silence followed. Brenda took a deep breath and said, "Yes, I am scared in here."

Other members of the group rushed in to diffuse the tension, assuring Brenda that there was nothing to fear and joking that no one would dare try to harm such a cute porcupine.

Disregarding the shallow reassurances of the group, I again turned my attention toward the image of the porcupine. "Porcupine, do you know what scares you about this forest?" I asked.

Brenda thought for a moment and said: "People may not agree with me, but I think this forest is an illusion. It's all just pretending."

The woman who'd drawn the apple tree responded: "Of course we are pretending. We can't really be trees and animals; this is just silliness."

Brenda turned toward her peer and replied: "That's the trouble, isn't it? We are all just faking it all the time." Tears formed in her eyes and she continued: "Here we are in a program because our lives are a mess, and we sit around and act like this is some kind of a party or something. You might not want to hear it but, yes, I am scared. I am scared to death that I don't even know what is real anymore."

The group was never the same after that session. The metaphors of the forest and Brenda's frightened porcupine prompted the group to decide to genuinely engage in therapy.

The Importance of the Therapeutic Alliance in Metaphorical Work and Treatment Planning

Establishing a positive therapeutic alliance between therapists and clients is always important. When art therapists use therapeutic metaphors, empathy is essential to treatment. The existence of a therapeutic alliance denotes an empathic relationship marked by an atmosphere of safety, trust, and understanding between parties involved.

When a positive therapeutic alliance is securely established, art therapists can engage clients in metaphoric communication, be it fantastic, outrageous, or thinly disguised, and this communication is accepted as a part of the therapeutic process. If rapport has not been established, clients may reject metaphoric communication as meaningless or nonsensical.

Two primary categories of techniques art therapists use exist to foster positive therapeutic alliances with clients: unspoken and spoken. In therapy literature, attention is given to verbal rapport-building techniques, but in relation to art therapy, metaverbal unspoken messages may be more powerful than words. For all intents and purposes, any facet of an art therapist's metaverbal behavior may contribute to the development of a therapeutic alliance or, conversely, inhibit such development. Some important unspoken behaviors include: tone of voice; body posture and movements; personal appearance; and physical contact.

Tone of Voice

In interpersonal communication, how something is said is often at least as important as what is actually said. Everyone experiences occasions when other people's words don't match their facial expressions or tones of voice. Such experiences leave one unsure of what messages other people meant to convey. Therapists should consider how they use their voice to cultivate a therapeutic persona. Tone of voice and volume can convey acceptance, support, warmth, enthusiasm, and openness.

Body Posture and Movement

The way art therapists move in space, gesture, sit, and physically respond to clients can subtly promote rapport and aid the development of empathy within the therapist. In discussing therapeutic techniques that convey a sense of connection to clients, Barker (1996) suggests adopting a similar body posture to that of the person with whom you are interacting. "If that person leans forward, you should lean forward also; then, when the person settles back in the chair, you should settle back" (p. 78). Barker's physical mirroring process is a rapport-building technique.

In art therapy contexts, clients and therapists seldom sit still for extended periods. Art therapy is an active encounter, and thus, it behooves art therapists to consider how they could use their bodies to initiate and convey unspoken messages, rather than simply reflecting clients' movement and posture. For example, when working with art therapy groups, I often partially extend one arm with the palm of my hand upturned and open, and then make a sweeping motion with my arm while making eye contact with group members. The motion is a non-verbal call for member inclusion: a circling up of participants. The upturned palm is a gesture of offering and holding. The unspoken message to the group is "gather round, I am open to you, I have something to give you, and I will hold what you give to the group." My point is that in the therapeutic context, art therapists' bodies communicate behavioral metaphors that deserve serious consideration. Just as clients tell their stories partially through behavior, so, too, do art therapists.

Personal Appearance

The personal appearance of an art therapist conveys subtle and overt messages. There is no easy formula for how appearance effects rapport, and what works for one art therapist in one situation may not be appropriate for another. Many art therapists consider clothing and other aspects of physical appearance to be important expressions of personal identity. This may be because of their investment in their identity as artists. Art therapists often take pride in dressing and grooming in a unique manner with a distinctly individual flamboyance. While art therapists may perceive their clothing and physical appearance to be outward symbols of their creative and unique individualism, clients may view their clothes as unprofessional or be drawn to the eccentricities.

Whether one's appearance is conventional or conservative, or flamboyant or eccentric, one must consider the metaphoric messages appearance conveys. Art therapists must weigh the potential positive and negative effects of their personal appearance in relation to the establishment of rapport with clients.

Physical Contact

Physically touching clients can convey potent, often unpredictable messages in art therapy. Touch can build or destroy rapport. Some art therapists view touch as a normal human process, and regard the notion of abstaining from physical contact as unnecessarily cold and guarded. Other art therapists consider physical contact with their clients to be taboo. The decision to touch a client or the client's artwork is one that must be made thoughtfully with consideration given to the potential positive and negative ramifications. Touch can be misconstrued, and has potential legal and ethical ramifications if an art therapist is not careful. Ultimately, every art therapist needs to consider the use of physical contact because of the potential impact it can have on the therapeutic alliance.

Preparation

The simple act of the art therapist being punctual and well prepared for the therapy session sends a metaphoric message to the client about the art therapist's trustworthiness and commitment to the relationship. A client once told me, after nearly two years of therapy, that my being on time for every session was one of the most important things that transpired between us. I cannot overstate this: If clients have to stand outside the door or sit in an anteroom waiting for the art therapist to arrive, a message is conveyed that they are not a top priority. Furthermore, this behavior communicates that the therapist is unreliable and not to be trusted.

A positive therapeutic alliance develops when the right circumstances are in place. It is the art therapist's job to plan for, prepare, and create conditions that promote a therapeutic alliance.

THE ROLE OF SAFETY, PREDICTABILITY, AND ART MAKING IN THE THERAPEUTIC ALLIANCE

In Chapter IV, three attributes of the therapeutic studio—safety, predictability, and relationship-focused art making—were discussed in relation to successful therapy. These three core elements are also essential as art therapists work to establish rapport with clients.

Safety

No matter how skilled artists-therapists are, how pleasant their studios are, or how fine artistic materials are, if clients do not feel safe, no therapeutic alliance can form. Art therapists must think through how to establish a sense of safety in the art therapy studio, office, or group room. Art therapists can take many actions to make the art therapy milieu feel safe.

The art therapist's attitude toward clients is important in creating a safe atmosphere. Clients are often sensitive to unspoken nuances and energies they receive from the environment. Clients can sense if the therapist likes working with them, not necessarily because of anything the art therapist says, but because such core attitudes seep into the environment in subtle ways.

I find that clients thrive on the art therapist's commitment and enthusiasm for artistic expression. A positive sense of contagion is established in the environment when art therapists actively engage in their own expressive art tasks, and this contagion encourages clients to safely engage in the processes of artistic self-exploration and self-discovery.

Art therapists should also consider the effects of their use of language in fostering safety and developing a therapeutic alliance. Some art therapists are relaxed and informal in their use of language, while others prefer more formal language. For example, many art therapists encourage clients to address them by their first name. This is in contrast to other helping professions. In some settings, psychiatrists and physicians are referred to by a formal title like Doctor. Either way of being addressed can promote safety and facilitate rapport, but a different relational context is established depending on the language used.

Excessive informality in art therapy contexts can undermine the development of therapeutic relationships (Moon, B. L., 2005). Some art therapists strive to establish a non-authoritarian, non-hierarchical relationship with clients. Therapy relationships, however, are not synonymous with personal friendships (Moon, B. L., 1998). Using appropriate professional language can counteract clients' attempts to relate to art therapists as if they were friends instead of experts. Similarly, art therapists should avoid using slang and profanity, which can create a false sense of familiarity that may be detrimental on the art therapy relationship.

Predictability

For clients to successfully engage in art therapy, they must perceive the art therapist as safe and predictable. The art therapist's predictability is prominent in the client's experience of safety. The art therapist must be committed to constructing and maintaining a consistent, predictable therapy milieu capable of holding unpredictable discoveries in the client's artistic efforts. It is impossible for art therapists to know exactly what will happen in therapy, but they can be reasonably sure about how to respond to what occurs.

Art therapists can establish themselves as predictable forces in clients' lives in many ways. Among the behaviors art therapists can engage in are: being punctual; welcoming the client into the therapeutic space the same way each session; providing necessary art supplies and tools; displaying consistency in affect and attitude; consistently working on personal art as a part of the therapy process; consistently responding to clients' behaviors; and developing and adhering to rituals that begin and end sessions. Predictability is important because many of the clients who enter art therapy bring with them personal histories in which significant people in their lives were unpredictable and untrustworthy.

Making Art to Establish Relationships

One of the most enriching gifts art therapists offer clients is art making. Many therapy disciplines–psychiatry, psychology, social work, counseling, and ministry–have inherent limitations that stem from their verbal nature. Art therapy has the unique advantage of being able to engage clients through visual, tactile, kinetic, and aural means. In addition, art-making processes involve clients and art therapists in tasks that incorporate ideas, feelings, and physical sensations. None of the verbally oriented therapy disciplines have such easy access to all these possibilities.

The unique sensual characteristics of art therapists' work with clients are tied to artistic activity. Therefore, as one considers the development of the therapeutic alliance, special attention is given to making art as an experience that fosters relationships. The therapeutic alliance is fostered when focus is placed on the mutual experience of an art process, such that the therapeutic relationship emerges from the shared experience of the client and therapist making art together. Making art is not merely a means to establish relationships; rather, art making is the ground from which relationships grow. Art therapists build relationships through their willingness to engage in art processes with clients. There is an elegant reciprocity in this: On one hand, art making creates a milieu in which relationships grow; on the other hand, relationships provide a fertile ground from which images emerge.

SUMMARY

It is important for art therapists and clients to share a clear vision of the desired therapeutic outcome. The art therapy treatment plan is intended to be a road map that predicts the course of clients' progress from where they are at the beginning of therapy to where they want to be at the end. Striving to develop a coherent treatment plan, art therapists must also contend with the reality that much of what occurs in the art therapy studio resists premeditation.

Constructing the therapeutic alliance is a critical step in the early stages of art therapy, but it is also an ongoing process that deserves serious attention. As Barker (1996) notes, "Rapport can be destroyed just as it can be fostered" (p. 80). The success of the therapy process hinges on the art therapist's ability to build a therapeutic alliance with the client. This alliance, marked by an atmosphere of safety, trust, and understanding, is essential to metaphorical art therapy.

Chapter X

RITUAL AS ENACTED METAPHOR

Rituals are enactments of metaphors performed in a set, ordered, and ceremonial way. Ritual actions communicate information and reinforce social cohesion. People perform rituals in order to symbolize essential truths of existence (Campbell, 1968; Moon, B. L., 1990, 1995). All societies develop rituals that serve as psychological or spiritual indicators, or both, of significant milestones in people's lives. Baptisms, coming-of-age initiations, weddings, divorce ceremonies, and funerals all mark important occasions laden with developmental, psychological, communal, and spiritual meanings.

An example of an important ritual in Christian religious communities is the Eucharist. The sacramental action of breaking bread is a visible translation of the metaphor of Jesus' brokenness. This brokenness is interpreted in different ways by various denominations within Christianity, but partaking of communion is a central organizing event in most congregations regardless of their denominational interpretation of the meaning of the rite.

In the United States, many ceremonial events and national observances focus on citizenry and inspire contemplation of shared experiences. These range from the somber ritual of the changing of the guard at the Tomb of the Unknown Soldier and hope-filled annual replaying of Martin Luther King's (1963) *I Have a Dream* speech, to the celebratory display of fireworks on the 4th of July.

Sporting events incorporate ritualized coin tosses, first pitches, and end-of-game handshakes. I know that fall is here when college football kicks off a new season, and that spring is almost here when the green jacket is presented at the close of the Master's golf tournament.

Rituals give visible structure to important phenomena in cultures, organizations, communities, families, and individuals. It is no surprise that rituals as enactments of metaphoric themes are often helpful in therapy and beneficial in times of transition in clients' lives. Of course therapy itself is often a significant transitional phase in people's lives. Clients typically seek art therapy in some state of distress, which is often caused by emotional, physical, spiritual, or circumstantial factors. Regardless of the nature of the discomfort, clients embark on the art therapy journey in hopes that changes will occur. Thus, therapy is a transition point: the end of one chapter and beginning of another.

As I gather art materials and prepare the studio prior to sessions, I engage in the ritual of making ready. Whether I'm positioning chairs in a circle, arranging brushes and paint jars, placing canvases on easels, or taping blank paper to the wall, my actions help me focus on what will come. These actions assist my process of preparatory emptying, letting go of outside distractions, and opening up to clients.

In the same way, at the end of sessions, after clients leave the studio, I participate in rituals of closure: cleaning brushes, scraping paint smears from the table, scouring the sink, and sweeping the floor. These actions provide a transitional experience through which I shift from the intensity of client encounters to the reality of my own day. As paint and water swirl into the drain, and chalk dust and paper scraps are emptied from the dustpan to the wastebasket, I participate in a ritual of letting go.

Between rituals of preparation and closure, clients and I engage in art tasks that actively translate the metaphors of their lives into visible objects. Hence, the act of making art is a ritual of self-exploration, self-expression, and self-discovery.

Jill and her Water

Not long ago, several of my students, fellow members of the faculty, and I attended the opening colloquium sponsored by the graduate art therapy program. The colloquium convenes each fall semester at a YWCA camp in the woods of southern Wisconsin for a weekend immersion in art making. The goal of this learning community event is to set the emotional and intellectual tone for the academic year.

During the first evening of the colloquium, Jill, a second-year student, made a self-deprecating joke about her inability to draw or paint anything other than water scenes. "I've really got water on the brain these last few months," she admitted. I had noticed that water themes were recurrent in her artworks the preceding spring semester.

As the colloquium proceeded, Jill continued to make artworks featuring water. She also seemed to become increasingly irritable and agitated as the weekend progressed.

As students were sitting around the lunch table in the main lodge at the camp, Julie, one of Jill's peers, made what seemed to be a benign comment about Jill's "precipitation preoccupation." Jill snapped at Julie and abruptly left the lodge.

Several minutes later, walking from the main lodge to the building we were using as an art space, I came upon a tearful Jill. She told me that she was embarrassed by her behavior. "I'm just under so much stress," she said. "I know Julie was just kidding around. I don't know why it bothered me so much."

On Saturday night, near the end of the colloquium, students participated in an evening of performance art, in which they could choose to actively engage as artists or be members of the audience. I was somewhat surprised that Jill volunteered to create a performance artwork. Since she seemed so irritable and complained about stress, she could have easily taken the more passive position as a member of the audience.

Jill's performance piece was gracefully simple. At the beginning, she slowly walked to the middle of the stage carrying a glass pitcher of water and large wooden bowl. She stared into the empty space above the heads of the audience and proceeded to pour water from the pitcher into the bowl. When the bowl was full, she gently placed the pitcher on the floor and poured water from the bowl back into the pitcher. She then paused, directed her gaze toward the pitcher, and said, "Slow down, forgive, breathe." Jill repeated this sequence of events seven or eight times in a performance that lasted nearly 10 minutes. The affect on the audience was mesmerizing, and when Jill said "breathe" for the last time, I heard many inhalations and exhalations (including my own).

At the end of the performance, members of the audience were encouraged to give the artist feedback. Jill's peers offered many positive reviews and speculations on the meanings of the performance. Though she neither confirmed nor denied her peers' interpretations of her work, Jill experienced a shift in affect and in her peers' responses to her. Clearly she was forgiven as she allowed herself to slow down and breathe.

Chapter XI

METAPHORIC INTERVENTION

In preceding chapters, I discuss the idea that all images clients create are metaphoric of the artist's life. I explore a range of metaphoric forms of expressions including: verbal metaphors, visual metaphors, and kinetic metaphors. I also include clinical vignettes illustrating art therapist's metaphoric interactions with clients and metaphoric responses to clients' images.

In this chapter, I explore the use of metaphoric interventions generated by the art therapist. Well-timed metaphoric stories, actions, and images can sometimes reach particular clients in ways that logical verbal interaction or cognitive behavioral therapy cannot.

My therapeutic interactions with Mariah, an adolescent client diagnosed with borderline personality disorder, are an example of a therapist-generated metaphoric intervention. When Mariah was referred to my art therapy group, she had been an inpatient on the adolescent unit of a psychiatric hospital for several weeks. For over a year prior to coming to the hospital, Mariah had been treated in a number of other residential facilities. Despite her extensive treatment history, she was aloof and detached from the treatment staff, and yet she demanded interaction with her caregivers through self-mutilating behaviors. She frequently engaged in self-cutting, and her forearms bore gruesome testimony to the intensity of her inner struggle. At the time of her referral to the art therapy group, members of the treatment team were concerned that she remained distant from the staff and showed no signs of meaningful attachment toward her individual psychotherapist.

For the first several sessions in the adolescent art therapy group, Mariah participated in the art tasks, but abstained from verbal interaction with her peers or me. Although she created several expressive and provocative images, she never commented on her drawings. I believe the most important work a client does in art therapy is manifested in the creation of art, and that conversations about artworks in a group setting can help build group cohesion, identify similarities among group members, and express support and concern for others.

In that particular group, the normative behavior was to create an image and discuss it with group members. After all members of the group completed their artworks, we would sit in a circle and talk about their creations. Clients could say as little or as much as they wished about their artworks, but Mariah's said nothing about hers, which was atypical in the group.

During this phase of her treatment, when it was Mariah's turn to discuss her image, I would say, "Mariah, would you like to share anything with the group about what you have drawn?"

She would roll her eyes in scorn, sigh, and look away. Rather than confront her resistance directly, I would make simple comments like, "Trust me, Mariah." Then I would move on.

As the weeks passed, Mariah began to offer comments about others' artworks; still, she remained doggedly unwilling to talk about her creations. After many sessions marked by Mariah's minimal verbal involvement, I decided to share a story with the group. The story was a variation of an extended metaphor that I occasionally share in art therapy groups in hopes that it convey a message to the group as a whole (and in this instance to Mariah in particular) regarding the nature of trusting relationships:

> Once upon a time, there was a lonely man who longed for a pet. He considered going to the animal shelter and adopting a puppy or kitten, but somehow the thought of going to the shelter was overwhelming. He worried that he would not be able to choose from all the animals there, and this made him sad. He would often walk into the local pet store and look at all the animals-gerbils, parakeets, white mice, and goldfish–but he couldn't make up his mind.
>
> One day, as he ambled through a park, he saw a gray rabbit by a bush. The rabbit appeared to be so small and vulnerable,   and was all alone in the park. "Aha," the man said to himself, "a rabbit! That's what I want to be my pet." He walked toward the rabbit, but when he got too close, it hopped away. "Come back," he pleaded. "I will not hurt you," he said. But the rabbit had disappeared into the brush. This made the man sad, and he felt even lonelier than before.

Then he had an idea. He went to a sporting goods store and bought a fisherman's net. When he walked in the park the next day, he saw the rabbit eating near the same bush. He lunged toward the rabbit and swung his net, but the rabbit was startled and darted away into the underbrush.

That night, undaunted, the man constructed a rabbit trap using a cardboard box, some string, and a stick. Early the next morning, he positioned the trap by the bush in the park and placed a carrot under the box as bait. The bunny, however, smelled the scent of the man and did not approach the carrot.

The man was unhappy. The next day he went to the park, sat down on the grass, and just watched the rabbit as it ate and scampered about. The man did this for several days in a row. With each day, the bunny inched closer to the man. At last, one wonderful day, the rabbit crept so close it nuzzled the man's hand.[1]

When I finished the story, I asked group members to draw their responses to it. Mariah drew a cartoon of several people sitting together under a large tree. When it was her turn to talk about her drawing, she looked at the cartoon and said, "This is supposed to be us; I think I trust you guys."

My purpose in telling the story of the man and rabbit was to subtly convey the sense of frustration I felt in trying to engage Mariah, and yet I wanted to also assure her that I would wait for, not abandon, her. Her response showed that she understood this metaphoric intervention.

The proceeding art therapy group sessions with Mariah were like games of chess. Each of her moves tested my trustworthiness and the group's dependability. My responses to her were intended to counter her suspicions and fears. From time to time, she would skitter off into her emotional thicket. These times, I would lament that I could not build the perfect rabbit trap.

The metaphor of the rabbit and man became a recurrent image in Mariah's therapy. References to the story reminded her that I would not (could not) build a trap large enough or clever enough to catch her against her will. Allusions to the story conveyed the message that I was willing to be patient, sit with her, and wait until she was ready to approach the difficult work of therapy.

---

1. This story appears in a slightly altered form in *Existential art therapy: The canvas mirror* by B. L. Moon, 1990 and 1995.

The Story of Darren and Eli's Hall of Reflection

Another example of a therapist generated metaphoric intervention was seen in my interactions with Darren, a middle-aged sales representative. He was referred to my private practice after several bouts of chest pains and anxiety attacks that resulted in trips to the emergency room, in which each time he was in perfect physical health. Darren was convinced that the doctors were wrong, and that he would soon die.

Like many good sales representatives, Darren attempted to anticipate the needs of everyone around him. He had been promoted steadily within his company and, at that time, was responsible for a large sales region. With each promotion, the demands on his time and energy increased, which caused tension between himself and his wife, and distanced him from his family. The tension at home inhibited his performance at work, which made him want to work even harder, and resulted in even more emotional and physical distance from his wife. On and on the cycle went. As his family relationships and job performance deteriorated, his supervisor exerted more pressure on him, and this exacerbated the difficulties. Darren sought comfort in a friendship with an attractive colleague at work, and eventually had an affair with her that left him feeling guilty, isolated, and trapped.

In one of his early art therapy sessions, Darren responded to the directive "draw yourself where you are" by creating an image of himself "lost in a maze." The problem," he said, "is that I can't remember how I got here, much less how to get out."

I looked at his drawing and wondered, "What's it like to be in the maze all alone?"

Darren responded by telling a story about a camping trip he went on when he was a teenager, during which he had gotten temporarily lost in the woods. He made a joke about needing a GPS system, but he did not identify any feelings. As I sat with him that day, I sensed that he really was lost, and desperately out of touch with his feelings and needs. He was truly alone in a maze of his own making.

In subsequent sessions, whenever I encouraged him to express his feelings, he would quickly assume his sales representative persona, and offer humorous stories and platitudes, but no feelings.

After several sessions that did not seem particularly helpful to Darren, I began an art therapy session by telling this story:[2]

---

2. Hall of Reflection, an original story by Moon, B., 2006.

Long ago, in the Land of All Seriousness, there was a man named Eli, who was accused of, tried for, and convicted of the crime of prevarication. In that place and time, few crimes were considered more heinous by the populace than that of prevarication. The judge in the case sentenced Eli to an indefinite stay in the dreaded Hall of Reflection.

Eli was dragged to his room in the Hall of Reflection, kicking and screaming all the way. "I didn't do it," he yelled. "I tell you, I've done all the right things, and I have never avoided anything in my entire life!" Over and over, he shouted, "I'm innocent," as the hall guard slammed the door. Feeling angry, miserable, and alone, Eli did not notice that the four walls of his room were covered from floor to ceiling with mirrors.

A harsh voice from the next room called out: "Yeah, we're all innocent in this joint. I've been locked up here on a trumped up charge for 10 years now, and I am as blameless as the judge himself–maybe more so!"

Eli took no comfort in his neighbor's words and he yelled louder. After a few days of shouting himself hoarse about his innocence, Eli settled in to a routine that divided his time between ruminating over the injustice of it all and making plans for getting the truth of his innocence before the right people. He spent many hours daydreaming about how embarrassed the judge would be hand-delivering a President's pardon to Eli's room. The judge would stutter, stammer, and blush in misery and self-reproach over having locked up such a noble, forthright and virtuous man. Eli imagined keeping a stoic expression on his face as the authorities renounced his conviction. On behalf of the President, the judge would offer elaborate incentives to appease Eli: a new car, fine house in the country, and appointment to be CEO of a prosperous corporation.

Eli decided he would sue the judge to avenge the injustice that had been inflicted on him. Eli's eyes lit the darkness of his cell as he rehearsed the mental scene of the day when his innocence would win out. He played, and replayed these scenes in his mind, but he never once noticed the mirrored walls of his room.

In the meantime, Eli did what he could to pass time in the Hall of Reflection. He wrote long letters to the authorities and shouted his innocence to everyone who passed his cell.

Eli had been incarcerated for several years, when one day, while taking a break from writing a letter to his lawyer, with his throat sore from shouting and his eyes tired, he glanced at the wall beside his bed. He dropped his pen and stared. There, looking straight at him. was a man Eli could hardly recognize. He knew that he was seeing his own reflection, but the man in the mirror was unfamiliar. He looked miserable, tired, and lonely, and not at all innocent. Eli stared. His righteous anger at the authorities melted away, and he was suddenly filled with despair. How could the man in the mirror be his own reflection? "What have I done," he asked himself. "What have I become? Who am I?"

Over the next few days, Eli spent fewer hours writing letters, fantasizing about revenge, and shouting about his innocence. In place of these activities, he simply looked into the mirror and asked himself questions. In the ensuing days, he quit writing letters, ceased his shouting, and gave up daydreaming about the judge.

As usual one evening, the hall guard brought Eli's meal. "Dinner is served, Mr. Innocent," he said as he lowered the tray toward the slot in the mirrored door.

Eli was sitting in his chair, looking at the wall and thinking about his life. Absentmindedly, he sighed and said, "Thank you for bringing my dinner, but I've been doing a lot of thinking, and I'm not innocent."

The hall guard was stunned and he sounded excited when he asked, "What's that you say?" To Eli, the guard seemed to be holding his breath, waiting for an answer.

Again, Eli sighed and said, "I've been doing a lot of thinking and looking at myself, I said."

The hall guard dropped the dinner tray and immediately fumbled for his key ring, and rattled the key in the lock. As Eli watched, the door to his room opened slightly and the guard hurried away. He stood up and tentatively gave the door a shove. It swung open into the abandoned hallway.

Looking cautiously down the hall, Eli saw that all of the other mirrored doors were also opened wide before him all the way to the front entryway. There was just enough daylight left to allow a glimpse of the darkening blue sky and green grass that waited outside the main gate.

As I finished the story, tears were welling Darren's eyes. I said, "Before we talk about the story, let's draw a response."

Darren drew a picture of himself facing his wife, children, secretary, and boss. I asked him to share what he could about this drawing, and Darren said: "I have to tell them. I have to let them know: let them all know who I am, what I want, and what I really feel."

Darren continued weekly art therapy for several months after that session. Over time, he created a number of artworks that helped him redefine his life. In retrospect, had I coaxed, confronted, or strategically maneuvered Darren in an effort to help him express his feelings, I wouldn't have gotten far. The metaphoric account of Eli and his reflection, provided a poignant comparison that allowed Darren to identify his feelings and experience emotional liberation.

A Failed Metaphoric Intervention

Not every metaphoric intervention leads to positive outcomes, such as those illustrated in the vignettes of Mariah and Darren. Sometimes clients are not yet psychologically ready to understand or interpret the indirect messages of a therapist's metaphors. In such instances, the indirectness of metaphoric communication serves an important protective function in that no harm comes to the relationship as a result of the intervention. This is in contrast to mistimed direct confrontations or therapist's interpretations that sometimes leave clients feeling angry or misunderstood.

A defensive young adult client, Daniel, repeatedly made impulsive choices in relationships with girlfriends that led to negative consequences. Whenever I tried to logically discuss with him how his behavior was harmful to these relationships, he would immediately become hostile and guarded. During one therapy session, in an effort to indirectly intervene in his self-defeating behavior, I told a story about a bull in a field who wanted to get into an adjoining field where a number of cows were grazing. I said: "The bull was so focused on getting to the field that he kept ramming his head into the stone wall. He did this so many times that he finally knocked himself unconscious. When the bull regained consciousness, the cows had all moved on. It would have been easier if he had just walked to the gate. The gate was not bolted, and the bull could have easily nudged it open."

When I finished the story, Daniel looked at me with a blank expression and said, "Nice story, but what does that have to do with anything?" He clearly did not grasp the intended meanings of the metaphoric intervention. While the story of the bull did not lead Daniel to insights about his behavior with women, it did not result in a defensive reaction either. During a session several weeks later, Daniel and I were working on drawings as Elvis Presley's rendition of the song *Fools Rush In* (Mercer & Bloom, 1940) came on the radio:

> *Fools rush in, where wise men never go*
> *But wise men never fall in love*
> *So how are they to know*

Daniel turned to me and said, "That song reminds me of me."

Recalling the metaphor I'd introduced weeks earlier, I replied, "It reminds me of the bull who beat his head against the wall."

Daniel laughed and said, "I wish I'd known the gate wasn't locked."

* * * * *

Metaphoric stories, actions, and images generated by art therapists can reach clients in ways that logical verbal interactions cannot. When art therapists use metaphoric interventions, they must assess clients' responses. Therapeutic metaphors always operate at both conscious and unconscious levels. Barker (1985) notes that while the client may consciously attend to the apparent or superficial meaning of a story or image, the therapist hopes that the client's unconscious will respond to deeper metaphorical meanings (p. 206). Because of the indirect nature of metaphors, art therapists need to assess the unconscious responses of the client.

Art therapists are uniquely equipped to monitor the unconscious processes of clients because such information is almost always presented through nonverbal or metaverbal means. Indeed, much of the focus of art therapy is on things that cannot be spoken. In order to evaluate clients' responses to therapist-generated metaphors, the art therapist must consider: (1) clients' attention to the metaphor; (2) changes in clients' nonverbal communications; and (3) changes in clients' behaviors.

The initial quality an art therapist makes note of regarding a client's response to a metaphoric intervention is the amount of attention the client gives the metaphor. Is the client interested in the therapist's metaphoric image or story? If the client's attention is elsewhere, the response to the art therapist's metaphor is likely to be unsatisfactory. The second area of focus is on any observable change in a client's non-verbal communications. Shifts in posture, facial expression, bodily movements, and gestures can signify unspoken responses to the art therapist's metaphoric intervention. Finally, art therapists must be alert to changes in client's behaviors in response to metaphoric interventions. Ultimately, the purpose of therapy is to produce behavioral changes that reflect how clients feel about themselves, their relationships, and the world.

EPLILOGUE

E ven in the best of circumstances, communication between human beings is multilayered and complex. But people who come to art therapists are seldom in the best of circumstances. Often, art therapy clients are people who have difficulty expressing feelings and ideas directly. When art therapists enter therapeutic relationships, they commit to getting involved in the intricacies and complications of the communication process. When I met with an adolescent client for the first time during a 90-minute session, he said a total of two things: "Yeah" and "Uh huh."

The focus of this book is metaphoric communication that takes place among art therapists, clients, and images. Metaphoric artworks, stories, and actions are the tools of an art therapist's trade. I recall when Cathy and I were building our log home 20 years ago, after the foundation and sub-floor were in place, the first thing we put up was the front door. Every other aspect of the house depended on proper placement of the door. We measured, checked, and measured again before nailing the doorframe into place.

Like log house builders, art therapists, must know where to place the door in order to construct a safe therapeutic space for clients to freely explore how their lives fit together. This book on the role of metaphor in art therapy is little more than a tape measure intended to help art therapists gauge where to place the door. Metaphors in art therapy are primary openings into the lives of our clients. (How's that for a metaphor?) I hope that this book inspires art therapists to think deeply about the roles that metaphors can play in their approaches and responses to clients and clients' artworks.

This book offers examples and ideas that I hope art therapists will adapt for their own use. The problems and difficulties people bring to us are too complicated and varied for a cookbook approach, so I avoid giving recipes. Rather, I hope that this text serves as a starting point, a doorway from which art therapists can construct their own unique therapeutic houses. In using this book as a philosophic guide, attending to details is important. As a carpenter friend told me when we were building the house, "Measure twice, cut once." In art therapy, details are the artworks created by our clients; words said; movements, gestures, and facial expressions made; sounds heard; and rituals enacted. In this book, I discuss pilots who failed to understand, footballs recalling past glory and disappointment, lighthouses that guided lost kids through storms, foghorns, wounded trees, empty fields, shy bunnies, mirrored walls, and house building. Potential metaphors are all around us. Everywhere art therapists look, metaphors wait to engage us, inviting us to build deeper therapeutic relationships with clients.

REFERENCES

Allen, P. B. (1995). *Art is a way of knowing.* Boston: Shambhala. The American Heritage Dictionary of the English Language. (1969). Boston: Houghton Mifflin.

American Psychiatric Association. (2000). *Diagnostic and statistical manual of mental disorders* (4th ed). Washington, DC: Author.

Arnheim, R. (1966). *Toward a psychology of art.* Los Angeles: University of California Press.

Barker, P. (1985). *Using metaphors in psychotherapy.* New York: Brunner/Mazel.

Barker, P. (1996). *Psychotherapeutic metaphors: A guide to theory and practice.* New York: Brunner/Mazel.

Campbell, J. (1968). *The masks of God: Creative mythology.* New York: Penguin Books.

Crosby, D. (1967). Mind Gardens. On *Younger than yesterday* [Record album]. New York: Sony.

Dewey, J. (1934). *Art as experience.* New York: Milton Balch.

Dylan, B. (1966). *Sad-eyed lady of the lowlands.* On Blonde on Blonde, LP. New York: Columbia Records.

Frost, R. (1920). The road not taken. In *Mountain interval.* New York: Henry Holt and Company.

Gussow, A. (1971). *A sense of place: The artist and the American land.* San Francisco: Friends of the Earth.

Haley, J. (1973). *Uncommon therapy: The psychiatric techniques of Milton H. Erikson, MD.* New York: Norton.

Haley, J. (1976). *Problem-solving therapy.* New York: Harper & Row.

Hillman, J. (1989). *A blue fire.* New York: Harper & Row.

Jones, G. W. (1969). *The innovator.* Nashville, TN: Abingdon Press.

King, M.L. (1963). *I have a dream.* Speech delivered at the Lincoln Memorial, August 28, 1963, Washington, DC.

Kopp, R. R. (1995). *Metaphor therapy: Using client-generated metaphors in psychotherapy.* New York: Brunner/Mazel.

Kopp, S. B. (1972). *If you meet the Buddha on the road, kill him.* New York: Bantam Books.

Kopp, S. B. (1976). *Guru.* Palo Alto, CA: Science and Behavior Books.

Kreiger, R. & Morrison, J. (1967). Light my fire. On *The Doors*, LP. New York: Elektra.

Leiber, J. & Stoller, M. (1997). *Lieber and Stoller songbook.* NY: Hal Leonard Publishing Corp.

Lowenfeld, V., & Brittain, W. L. (1970). *Creative and mental growth* (5th ed.). New York: Macmillan.

McNiff, S. (2004). *Art heals: How creativity cures the soul.* Boston: Shambhala.

Mercer, J., & Bloom, R. (1940). *Fools rush in.* New York: VG-Bregman, Vocco and Conn.

Moon, B. L. (2005). *Ethical issues in art therapy* (2nd ed.). Springfield, IL: Charles C Thomas.

Moon, B. L. (2004). *Art and soul: Reflections on an artistic psychology* (2nd ed.). Springfield, IL: Charles C Thomas.

Moon, B. L. (1998). *The dynamics of art as therapy with adolescents.* Springfield, IL: Charles C Thomas.

Moon, B. L. (1997). The gate is not burning. *Proceedings of the AATA National Conference.* Mundelein, IL.

Moon, B. L. (1990, 1995). *Existential art therapy: The canvas mirror.* Springfield, IL: Charles C Thomas.

Moon, C. (2002). *Studio art therapy: Cultivating the artist identity in the art therapist.* London: Jessica Kingsley.

Papini, G. (1934). *A visit to Freud,* reprinted in *Rev. Existential Psychology and Psychiatry, IX* (1969): pp. 130–134.

Pfeiffer, J. W., & Jones, J. E. (1981). *A handbook of structured experiences for human relations training.* La Jolla, CA: University Associates.

Phillips, R. (1988). The creative moment: Improvising in jazz and psychotherapy. *Adolescent Psychiatry.* Chicago, IL: The University of Chicago Press.

Springsteen, B. (1977). Fire. On *Live 1975–1985,* LP. New York: Columbia Records.

Webster's New World Dictionary: 3rd college edition. (1988).
    New York: Simon and Schuster.

Whyte, D. (1994). *The heart aroused: Poetry and the preservation of the soul in corporate America.* New York: Currency Doubleday.

INDEX

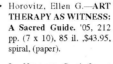

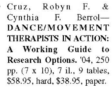
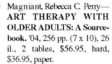
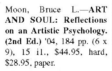